Take Me with You

"I first heard Scott Jackson's story when he shared it at the annual Strong Women, Strong World Summit in New York City. I have the privilege of serving as a Global Celebrity Ambassador and spokesperson for World Vision and Strong Women, Strong World. Scott's beautifully written childhood story is one of struggle, perseverance and service to others. We share much in our journeys. We both grew up in the Midwestern United States during a time when political turmoil, challenges to faith, racial prejudice and the fight for civil rights served as our backdrop as they do today. As a mother of four I share Scott's belief that every woman and every child, regardless of their circumstances or where they were born, should have the opportunity to live their full potential. As an actress, storyteller, and global citizen I encourage everyone to accept Scott's call to action to 'Make a Global Impact' by sharing their story, committing their time, talent, and treasure to a cause they care about and becoming an advocate for a better world. Scott and I are passionately committed to Strong Women making a Strong World for all because we know that when women and girls are empowered everyone wins!!!"

—PATRICIA HEATON
Actress, World Vision Ambassador

"Scott Jackson knows that good storytelling helps people discover their passions and connect with great causes. In *Take Me with You*, he tells his own story, explaining how a child's decision to run away from an abusive father in the middle of a Kansas snowstorm changed his life and made him a fighter for justice and equity. Scott understands the power of the personal narrative, and he uses it to weave a compelling call to action to address the toughest development challenges of the 21st century."

—DR. CHRISTOPHER ELIAS
President of Global Development, Bill & Melinda Gates Foundation and founder and CEO of PATH

"From the moment I met Scott Jackson in the fall of 1976 my life has been enriched and inspired by his contagious energy and passion. Now *Take Me with You* inspires its readers. Scott Jackson's book is an important combination of call for action and a wonderful read that tells a meaningful story."

— **JOHN OPPENHEIMER**
CEO of Columbia Hospitality

"When Scott Jackson worked with me at World Vision, I saw his heart for vulnerable children before I knew his story—and what a remarkable story it is! A young white boy caught in the midst of racial discrimination and abuse in America's Midwest in the 1960s makes a daring cross-country escape to find a new life in an African-American community in the Pacific Northwest. Yet the things that could have broken him instead made him stronger in his faith, his compassion, and his desire to be a catalyst for justice. This book is a riveting and amazing read."

— **RICHARD STEARNS**
President Emeritus of World Vision U.S.

"*Take Me with You* spoke to my heart. Scott Jackson writes of growing up as a young White boy in the Midwest during the early 60s when communities across the United States were confronting the harsh realities of racial inequality. Scott lived just this side of the railroad tracks with an abusive father who crushed the very spirit of those he loved best: Scott and his mother. In their attempt to escape the terror of an abusive home, Scott and his mother sought physical and spiritual sanctuary within the Black community living on the other side of the tracks, and discovered pathways to healing that speak to humanity's great capacity for acceptance and compassion and, yes, love.

In a deceptively simple style, Scott recounts his journey with grace and humility. Through his story we come to appreciate that Scott, by virtue of his deep faith and unique life experiences, has been able to find 'the charity within.' How extraordinary to have woven his story as a survivor of abuse and as a kid growing up in a biracial family with insights gathered across the years working as a leader in global development and as an expert on US philanthropy! We should all thank Scott for writing

Take Me with You. Such an authentic voice is rare, and the promise of his story is one that we need to realize today. ”

    —SARAH DEGNAN KAMBOU
        President of the International Center
        for Research on Women

“Scott Jackson’s *Take Me with You* is an amazing tale that is truly made captivating by his early struggles with racism and how that shaped his commitment and career to serving others. As a child, he faced difficult choices involving his biological father and mother’s marriage to a Black preacher that complicated his life but eventually proved inspirational. Often it’s not the smooth sailing through life, but a tough and bruising journey that builds character and leads to higher achievements. Scott Jackson’s story is revealing of his spirit and determination to make a difference in people’s lives, clearly demonstrated throughout the book and by his senior executive positions with the world’s most prominent organizations. *Take Me with You* will bring value and inspiration to anyone who reads it.”

    —DON BONKER
        Former United States Congressman

Take Me with You

Take Me with You

My Story of
Making a Global Impact

REVISED EDITION

Scott Jackson

SelectBooks, Inc.
New York

This edition published by SelectBooks, Inc.
For information address SelectBooks, Inc., New York, New York.

First Edition

ISBN 978-1-59079-509-5

Library of Congress Cataloging-in-Publication Data

Names: Jackson, Scott, (Philanthropist), author.
Title: Take me with you / Scott Jackson.
Description: New York : SelectBooks, 2017.
Identifiers: LCCN 2016029245 | ISBN 9781590793923 (hardback)
Subjects: LCSH: Jackson, Scott, (Philanthropist) | Philanthropists--United
  States--Biography. | Fund raising--United States. | Leadership. | BISAC:
  BIOGRAPHY & AUTOBIOGRAPHY / Personal Memoirs.
Classification: LCC HV28.J33 J33 2017 | DDC 361.7/4092 [B] --dc23 LC record
available at https://lccn.loc.gov/2016029245

The following song lyrics in the book are used with permission and credited to the following owners of copyright:

"We've Come This Far by Faith," page 68, ©Manna Music, Inc. All rights reserved.

"I'll Fly Away," page 146, ©Albert E. Brumley & Sons. All rights reserved.

Book design by Janice Benight

Manufactured in the United States of America
10 9 8 7 6 5 4 3 2 1

This is my story, my song, dedicated to the Reverend Jefferson Jackson—
Beloved Pastor, Husband, and Father.

To Sydney, the love of Jefferson's life and my mom,
who never wavered in her commitment to "Take Me with You."

To all of us who persevere to find the "charity within,"
regardless of life's circumstances.

"Life's most persistent and urgent question is,
'What are you doing for others?'"

—Martin Luther King, Jr.

Contents

Preface

My family lived outside Kansas City, and for much of our time together my dad preached at Edwardsville Christian Church. We lived in the parsonage, a two-bedroom box just south of the railroad tracks that separated the White and Black parts of town. I grew up during the American Civil Rights Movement, a time when my family fell apart and my future became uncertain because of a struggle between my parents and their different ways of life. As the civil rights movement heated up, my mom crossed the tracks whenever she could. For that and for other indiscernible reasons, Dad abused her. My background was the same as thousands—even millions—of other at-risk youth like me who had to overcome barriers of race, religion, and broken families.

During the winter of my thirteenth year, I ran away from home on a cold night in early February and disappeared into a Kansas snowstorm. By running away, I found a new life, and this journey also marked a rebirth for my mom and for Jefferson Jackson, the Black Baptist minister with a tenth- grade education who fell in love with my mother. He became a father figure to me and raised me. In our lives together we were often in hiding and almost always impoverished. From this beginning it seemed unlikely I would achieve the kind of worldly success that most privileged people expect. But we had love and a dedication to each other that is the foundation of well-being.

Because of the influence of my parents and others as I grew up, I chose to support the causes for justice and well-being for people throughout the world. My story tells how my own difficult childhood brought me to the world of global development where I was given the opportunities to work with many others to change the world. My work has often been behind the scenes, with a focus on building partnerships, raising funds, advocacy, and visibility for those on the front lines.

My childhood escape from abuse has influenced my present work and driven my personal commitment to leave a lasting mark on humanity. My story is about one boy who chooses forgiveness and finding the charity or love within. This meant letting go of the anger and regret about what could have been and choosing the positive to be a force for good. This is the same choice we each must make if we are to respect all people regardless of gender, race, socio-economic position, family origin, where a person is born, or the circumstances in which they find themselves. Each of us can harness the power of our own personal struggles to influence others and to have our own impact on the world.

Many of the events I recount took place more than forty years ago but have shaped the man I have become. I'm the sum of my story, this memoir rooted in love, faith, and courage. We all have a story to tell.

I wanted to share my story because it has influenced my own commitment to help others realize their full potential and contribute to a better, safer world. My goal is to offer a message of hope and encourage you to embark on your own journey to serve others and spark positive change—in whatever way you can—because every life matters and there are so many in need around the globe.

As I write this, I have the privilege of serving as President and CEO of Global Impact. Global Impact's mission as a global non-profit organization is to "build partnerships and resources for the world's most vulnerable people." Our amazing staff is comprised predominately of talented Gen Xers and millennials. Together, with our board of directors and our partners, we are all about "growing global philanthropy" and supporting those organizations—public, private, and nonprofit—that tackle the world's most pressing problems.

Over the past 65 years, Global Impact has raised more than $2 billion, supports charitable ventures to inspire greater giving and receives funds from hundreds of thousands of donors, and has distributed contributions to thousands of charities here in the United States and around the world. The Global Impact charity alliance supports the work of more than 100 international nongovernmental organizations (INGOs), including UNICEF, Care, Heifer International, Save the Children, and World Vision. The resources we raise have contributed to meeting the needs of approximately 400 million people in as many as 200 countries.

Before joining Global Impact, my own career journey included holding leadership positions in global development in the public, private, and nonprofit sectors, including leadership positions with World Vision and PATH. The range of issues I have worked on include at-risk youth in America's largest cities and underserved rural communities; responding to 9/11 and Katrina; funding for new vaccine development, including for meningitis in Africa and malaria worldwide; raising funds and awareness for combating HIV AIDS; and responding to the Syrian refugee crisis and other displaced persons in communities around the world. I have worked on presidential campaigns, and I was a founding member as a nonprofit leader for the ONE Campaign to end extreme poverty and preventable disease by 2030. I have traveled and worked in more than 65 countries, opening up new markets, promoting international trade, responding to crises, and supporting long-term development. But before I chose this focus on social impact, I lived through a childhood of struggle and hardship and had to overcome adversity, which is why I feel so personally connected to this work.

Bono launching the ONE Campaign in 2004 in Philadelphia with Dikembe Mutombo in the background

Standing in Solidarity with the Black Community

As the leader of Global Impact, an organization committed to equity and justice, I am deeply aggrieved by the murders of George Floyd, Breonna Taylor, Aumaud Arbery, and the countless other individuals who have been victims of law enforcement violence and the institutional racism and oppression that has plagued the United States for more than 400 years. Our nation has erupted from the pain and anguish that racism still brings us today. On top of the COVID-19 global pandemic, it almost feels too much for many of us to bear, but we are in this together.

Living in Washington, DC, I am often compelled to visit the Martin Luther King Jr. Monument. MLK Day is an official holiday for Global Impact. The MLK Jr. stamp sits on my desk as a paperweight

Scott with President Clinton. *President Clinton presenting me with a Clinton Global Initiative Commitment to Action in 2005.*

embedded in a piece of white marble, not unlike the monument itself. The stamp was a gift from Sydney, my mom, when she was the supervisor of the Sequim post office, one of the many jobs she held as the breadwinner of our family.

Since I grew up during a time when prejudice was rampant, and the small town where we lived did not accept the interracial marriage between my mom and Jefferson Jackson, we were often ostracized. Because of the color of Jefferson's skin, the Sequim families didn't want their daughters to date me. Skin color has so often played a role in the inequality in our society and throughout the world.

On January 18, 2016, in recognition of MLK Jr. Day (not in celebration), twenty thousand people came together in the FEDEX field where the "Red Skins" play—a name that is accepted by too many and that is finally changing. They were there to protest the violence against people of color in the United States. Black Lives Matter took over and blocked the San Francisco Bay Bridge.

Immigration reform for men, women, and children from Central and Latin America can't get through Congress, partly because of our prejudice. Wikipedia lists 120 pages of atrocities against people of color over the past century. We elected a Black president only to find that many people treated him and his family without due respect for eight years, largely because of our prejudice.

I wasn't as active in the Obama Campaign for President as I had been in the Clinton presidential campaigns, but I had the privilege of taking Sydney and my daughter Lindsay to the 2008 Inauguration in Washington, DC. We stood underneath the Capitol and the inaugural podium. It was bitterly cold, but we listened proudly as the first African American president of the United States of America was sworn into office with his family looking on—we knew the world had changed and each of us had played a part. Four years later, I would take Lindsay, my twin daughters Haley and Allison, my friend John Oppenheimer, and his daughter Jeni, who was working with me at

Global Impact, to the second-term inauguration of President Barak Obama, perhaps just as unprecedented.

I didn't know what my life would be like when I pleaded to my mother, "Take me with you." But I'm so glad she did and that Jefferson Jackson was there to join us and change our lives forever, as part of our own extraordinary journey and our own contribution as an interracial family to defeat the history of prejudice in America.

Because of these experiences, I have chosen a career of stopping the cycles of abuse, racism, poverty, and inequality. To effect lasting change within our communities and around the world, we must work together to elevate and empower the oppressed. Global Impact, as an organization, is committed to equity and justice for all. We must continue to find ways to support one another and to work for a more diverse, equitable, inclusive, and just world. Global Impact's mission is to stand up for the world's most vulnerable, and we vow to do our part to build a brighter future for all. I hope that you will join us in this mission.

Will COVID-19 Lead to Global Empathy?

The world has been challenged with unprecedented crises in human health, social justice, and economic needs. The COVID-19 pandemic has affected each and every one of us and our families and loved ones. We've been confronted with tragic incidents resulting from our systemic racism, abuse, and injustice toward people of color and must search every intention and action if we are to seize this moment and become a more equitable and just world. As of the writing of this book, we are facing a severe economic downturn, which will further increase the economic gap between rich and poor, push significant numbers of people into extreme poverty, defined as those earning less than $2 a day, and make the ability to meet the Global Development goals for Sustainability much harder.

In 2019, we had visions of what 2020 would look like. We had plans and goals we were going to accomplish, not only as individuals, but also as businesses. In the philanthropy sector, giving was reaching all-time highs, as detailed by the recent Giving USA report. Giving had increased a total of 33 percent between 2010 and 2019, and was on track to continue its upward trend.

None of us imagined that the world would look the way it does now—with closed borders, overtaxed hospitals, families separated from loved ones, and populations that haven't left their homes for months at a time. As I write this, there are more than 113 million confirmed cases of COVID-19 worldwide, and more than 2.5 million deaths, with marginalized communities negatively impacted disproportionally. As countries are in the midst of cautiously implementing reopening procedures, many of us are anxious to go back to how things were. However, things will never be quite the same.

Whether many vaccines are developed to inoculate a high percentage of the population, or Covid-19 variants mutate to either less or more contagious forms and we face many spikes in cases, Covid-19 will have more than a short-term impact on the world.

Philanthropy will be different, and the world will be different. The critical question that remains is this: In what way?

The coronavirus pandemic is primarily a major global health crisis, but its reach extends even further. We need to recognize the long-term threat it poses to goals and to the progress we've made in reaching the world's most vulnerable. Five years ago, the Sustainable Development Goals (SDGs) were adopted by the 193 United Nations member states. These 17 goals focus on key areas of development that need to be reached to achieve a sustainable future for all by 2030. Now, the pandemic has put these goals in jeopardy, a fact illustrated when we look at two areas that are closely linked: poverty and hunger.

Global Goal Number 1 is "No Poverty." But around the world, businesses have closed their doors and many people have lost their jobs. These closures have brought economies everywhere to a halt. In May 2020, the World Bank revealed that the pandemic could push 60 million more people into extreme poverty, characterized as living on less than $1.90 a day. The pandemic is "erasing much of the recent progress made in poverty alleviation," according to World Bank President David Malpass.

Global Goal Number 2 is "Zero Hunger." Closures caused by the coronavirus have also affected borders and markets, leading to food shortages and price hikes. With job loss on the rise, so, too, is lack of income. As a result, people are struggling to feed their families. Before the pandemic hit, 820 million people suffered from hunger—now, according to the UN, that number is set to double as a result of COVID-19.

The effects of this viral disease are rippling out from its epicenter in global health to ignite other potential crises across the relief and development sector. With regional restrictions, economic downturns, and a shift in funding away from other causes into global health, the pandemic is impacting the world in many other ways. Now is the time to consider the broader repercussion of the pandemic and what actors across sectors and donors will do to mitigate the effect. As we continue to see the full extent of the impacts from COVID-19, the work of international nonprofits is more important than ever before.

Nonprofits are being forced to navigate a new landscape—one where funding may not be as readily available and strategies may need to be reevaluated. They are fighting to mitigate the effects of a pandemic that is also impacting their own lives, moving to remote offices and wrestling with personal challenges, such as prolonged separation from loved ones.

These are hard times, but the nonprofit sector, as always, remains resilient and strong—they have seen the need to find new and creative ways to serve people worldwide, and they are working to meet it. Around the world, charities are pivoting strategies and developing more flexible responses in order to keep providing vital support to the world's most vulnerable.

What we need to see is a change in philanthropy from all angles:

Charities: Flexibility during difficult times has always been crucial, but this necessity is being taken to new levels—and charities are responding. They are pivoting strategies, expanding programs, and working with corporations in new capacities to meet the unique type of aid needed.

Corporations: Workforces around the world are being heavily affected by the pandemic. It's more imperative than ever before that companies invest in social impact to protect employees, communities, and the world at large.

Individuals: All of these changes cited are important, but none of these approaches will work without the individual donor—and that is where I hope to see the biggest change occur. Donors are usually separated from the emergencies by oceans and continents. Thousands of miles create a clear dividing line between them and a potential crisis. But COVID-19 has illustrated that we are not as isolated as we thought. Something occurring in a remote village in China can rapidly reach over barriers to affect someone on the other side of the world.

Crises have always given birth to empathy, driving people to come together and become a force for change. This is especially true when crises hit closer to home—for example, with Ebola, people around the world were afraid, but the disease did not spread globally, so we saw limited reaction from donors. It was easier to separate from the reality of a situation. This coronavirus disease is different. Donors are witnessing the effects of a pandemic firsthand. Because of this, they are more likely to empathize with marginalized communities that are being hit particularly hard by the pandemic. I hope that this empathy leads more people to identify as global citizens, spur a call for change, and increase generosity for those in need around the world.

We are in unprecedented times, facing a global health crisis that has now impacted every area of our lives in a way we never could have expected. The needs for marginalized communities have increased dramatically. Will we, as global citizens, now connected by this pandemic in an unparalleled way, be able to respond in empathy with generosity? Will philanthropy be the catalyst of positive change in the midst of this new world in which we find ourselves?

We have experienced these crises together. The whole of humanity and the world has been affected. Each of us will forever have a 2020 lens as part of our individual and collective stories, and we all have a chance to make an impact—and not let this moment of hardship detour us from the important work that needs to be done. Rather, we must use our collective stories about what we have endured to choose to love our fellow humans, regardless of their race or where they are born. We must choose the love within; we must be intentional in our choice to be *the other* for those around us. We must use this moment to change the world for the better.

To Gulu

In late 2005, I led a humanitarian trip to central Africa. For nearly two decades, warlord Joseph Kony had been kidnapping, raping, and enslaving local children. The Acholi people of northern Uganda and South Sudan absorbed the brunt of Kony's genocide. More than a million Acholi lived in crowded refugee camps, their only hope of safety. Kony came at night, abducted boys into his army, raped girls, and left the worst victims maimed and beheaded. To avoid the slaughter, children from area villages left their homes to make their way to secure compounds in the city of Gulu. The "night walkers," as they were called, entered the city before dusk and left at first light. These were the lucky ones.

In Uganda, our group consisted of Rotarians, donors, and community leaders who wanted to witness World Vision's work. At the time, I was a senior vice president of World Vision, the world's largest nonprofit relief and development organization. From the capital city of Kampala, we boarded a chartered bus to Gulu, two hundred miles north. As we moved farther from the capital, the roads grew bumpier, cars became infrequent, and the landscape faded into rural settlements. At various points along the way, bicycles crowded beside us, and women circled us with baskets, overflowing in color, balanced perfectly on their heads. We encountered multiple checkpoints. As we crossed the halfway point, closer to Gulu than to Kampala, we knew Kony's army was near by the heightened presence of government troops. We distracted ourselves by thinking about the children of Gulu, the victims we hoped to help. The final checkpoint before we reached the city took a long time. Government soldiers surrounded the bus. Two boarded with machine guns. Eventually the roadblock opened. Nothing could have prepared us for what we were about to witness.

Gulu resembled a walled-in city—without an actual wall. In its attempt to protect inhabitants from Joseph Kony, the city had sealed itself off from the rest of the world. Driving toward our hotel, we saw signs of war on every block. Army transport trucks. United Nations Refugee Commission supply vehicles. World Food Programme ware-houses. And, of course, the large football field-like enclosures with makeshift barracks and floodlights where the night walkers would seek refuge. We spent the next several days observing the results of Kony's war. I met a young woman whose nose, arm, and breasts had been cut off, and I saw the love she carried for her son, the child of a man who had raped and maimed her.

I sat with the woman a long time. And as I listened to her story, her son played nearby. I hoped our presence comforted them. I also knew that I could never do enough. I could never restore life before the war. Maybe, though, I could help provide a new one.

During my visit to Uganda, our delegation decided to walk in solidarity with the night walkers. Just before dusk, the streets stood empty. Then faces began to appear in the twilight. They seemed to materialize from nowhere. Soon, a sea of children surrounded us. Thousands of bodies pushed against each other as we moved toward the stadium, the epicenter of safety. In the midst of the crowd, I felt a tug on my hand. I looked down and saw a young girl. She said her name was Rose, and she asked who I was and where I came from. She smiled at me, gave me her hand, and we moved together with the mass. Inside the stadium, high fences surrounded us and floodlights illuminated the compound.

Suddenly, a unified sound began to move through the crowd. A chorus of a thousand voices began to sing. I recognized the words. "Blessed assurance, Jesus is mine. Oh, what a foretaste of glory divine! . . . This is my story, this is my song, praising my Savior all the day long."

We used to sing the same song at Edwardsville Christian and Gethsemane Baptist church. Here in Gulu, surrounded by thousands of African children seeking safety, for the first time in many years, I thought about my own childhood.

Scott Jackson is my chosen name, not the one I was born with. I took the name of my stepfather, the Reverend Jefferson Jackson, a Black Baptist minister with a tenth-grade education. The story I want to tell happened more than forty years ago, but it has shaped the man I have become. I am no longer the blond-haired, blue-eyed, skinny child; I am a fifty-plus-year-old man. My story is one of abuse and of hope. It's a memoir about a white woman who finally escaped abuse and the Black Baptist minister who saved us both.

CHAPTER ONE

When I Was Little

Edwardsville, Kansas, brushes the western border of Kansas City. It's a sliver of a town hammered between busy railroad tracks and the Kansas River. I moved to Edwardsville with my parents when I was eight months old, shortly after Dad finished seminary and he took his first preaching job. The three of us lived in the church parsonage. The house stood half a block from the railroad tracks. When the trains came, and they came often, family photos rattled on the walls and the entire house shook. Some of the trains pulled two hundred cars and seemed to last forever. To this day, I remember how loud they were. Years later, I wondered if that's why so many secrets stayed in our household for so long—people just couldn't hear them.

The parsonage squeezed two bedrooms, a bathroom, living room, kitchen, and laundry room into six hundred square feet, if that. On most days, Dad walked the four blocks to church across the tracks and highway. Along the way, he passed the town's old city hall, a stone building erected just a few paces off the rail line in 1917. After work, Dad stopped at the post office and store, the town's two main attractions. What Edwardsville lacked in population and culture, it made up for in small-town convenience. In 1958, the year we moved to town, Edwardsville was eight square blocks and home to five hundred people. During the entire time we lived there, I don't think we ever locked our doors.

The parsonage where we lived in Edwardsville, Kansas

I got to know Edwardsville better than anyone. By the time I turned six, I had ridden my bike through every gravel alley in town too many times to count. My bike was one of the best gifts ever. Normally, I received my presents on Christmas Eve. I was an only child and I would always tell my mom I couldn't wait. She couldn't either. I had been hoping for a bicycle, and not just any bike. I wanted a two-wheeler banana seat, high-handle bars special. I had been off training wheels for a couple of years and was ready for a real bike. That Christmas Eve there were other presents nestled under the tree but no bicycle.

The next morning Mom woke me and said, "Hurry, Santa left one more present!"

We made our way out of the house, across the small snow-covered yard, and into the garage. There it rested: the bike of my dreams.

We opened the garage door and my dachshund Dewey and I took off. I thought of stopping by Jackie Shumaker's house or several other homes in the neighborhood, but I didn't have close friends. Not everyone wanted to spend time with the pastor's kid who wasn't that cool. But I didn't care—I had my new bike, my best friend, Dewey, and the cold air on my cheeks. I was so fast on that bike that Dewey had a hard time keeping up with his short, little legs.

The air was brisk and the gravel alleyways were frozen. Edwardsville was a small town, and I knew every street. When I got tired of riding, I hung out by the tracks. Sometimes I'd collect rusty rail spikes or pick wildflowers growing in the dirt. Other times, I'd sneak through a thicket of trees along the bank of the Kansas River and watch the water pass. In that part of the state, the river runs wide and slow on its way to Kansas City. As long as I stayed in Edwardsville, I felt safe, and I felt safest on my bike in the alleyways away from the little parsonage called home.

My other favorite place when I was little—the one I might not tell anyone about—was my mother's lap, which I crawled into whenever I could. The rocking chair was our favorite resting place. I can still remember the squeak, lift, and pull of the family rocker, a gift from Grandpa Hughes, and the floor lamp turned on next to the rocker in the evenings when we would read together. My mom smelled like the wildflowers in the Kansas countryside. She opened the worn cover of the dark blue book and read the stories and showed me pictures from the Bible.

My mom was beautiful. She had long brown hair, a slender neck, and extraordinary green eyes. One recurring dream I had as a child was seeing my mom on a street corner in a blue dress with a string of pearls around her neck. Her hair was naturally a dark brunette and styled like a movie star. She was in many ways an "Elizabeth Taylor" figure, always trying to do the right or proper thing but really only interested in being loved for who she was.

Baby Scott sitting on his mother's lap

Sydney Lou looking like a movie star of the 60s and changing her hair with the times

Mom liked living in Edwardsville because it was close to her parents. Grandma and Grandpa Hughes lived on the other side of Kansas City, across the Missouri state line. During my childhood, I spent every day with Mom. We'd hop in her white Volkswagen VW and drive to the end of some rural road or down a quiet highway. Sometimes we'd stop and stare across fields grown dense with sunflowers. If we stayed long enough, we could see the flowers' huge yellow heads turn with the sun. Mom liked getting away, but she almost always had a destination. More often than parking along the sunflower fields, we parked next to homes even smaller than our own. Inevitably, children would be running in the yard or sitting alone in the distance.

As a pastor's wife, Mom made it her job to help our poorest neighbors. In the great expanse of rolling hills and farm country I once called home, that meant Negroes. Just writing that word haunts my memory. I only use it now because in the place I grew up, in the time I grew up, that's what almost everyone called Black people, if not something worse.

That's how it was in Enid, Oklahoma, too, where Mom and Dad first met at Phillips University during auditions for *Family Portrait*, the opening play of Mom's freshman year. Phillips was the top college for members of the Disciples of Christ Church. Built in an old alfalfa field, the campus stood as a temple of higher education in a community otherwise ruled by farmhands. Huge dust clouds blow through Enid, Oklahoma, and when a dust storm hit, students covered their mouths with shirt collars or handkerchiefs and raced inside to avoid suffocating in clouds of wind-whipped dirt.

My mother, Sydney Lou Hughes, was the apple of her daddy's eye. Most folks called her father "Whitey," or if you didn't know him too well, Gilbert. Whitey was the consummate entrepreneur and salesman. He had three sisters and a brother named "Red," and Whitey helped to raise them all. Whitey, a towhead, and Red, a redhead, were inseparable. They were in business together until Red died from alcoholism. Whitey almost always wore a dark suit and tie, which set off his hair. It was so blonde it appeared white in the sun.

Whitey had more small businesses than anyone could count. He and my grandmother went bankrupt once during the Great Depression years, only to get back up on their feet and start again. Whitey was well connected to the business and political interests in Missouri.

Thanks to my grandmother, Pauline, Whitey became a God-fearing, church-going community leader. She had been a teacher from Branson, Missouri, and was known as "Dick" the tomboy. My Grandpa Gilbert fell in love with her and they married. One early morning soon after they were married, Whitey's friends and brother Red brought him home drunk. Pauline promptly told Whitey that if he ever got up that way again, he needn't come home. He never did, and he joined her in church on Sundays.

Whitey and Pauline had two natural children, Sydney Lou and Irwin. Years later, they adopted two more children, Patty and Ricky, who had been abandoned, and they helped to raise and put through school many more children along the way. Irwin was a sickly child and school came hard for him. Grandma nursed him to health and helped him with school, which left Sydney Lou often on her own. She was vivacious, gregarious, intelligent, creative, and just as quick as Irwin wasn't. She talked at six months and skipped kindergarten and first grade, starting school in the second grade.

Whitey's great joy in life was his daughter, Sydney Lou, my mom, and he did everything he could to spoil her and make sure that she knew she could do anything she took a mind to in the world. It took every ounce of discipline

Pauline could muster to keep Sydney from marrying a local boy and make sure she was sent off to a good Christian college, Phillips University. So off she went, leaving her high school sweetheart behind.

It wasn't long before my mom fell for her future husband. She found Dad funny and good-looking. Back in college, he still had a medium build with large shoulders, a round face, and dark brown eyes that matched his black hair. He was popular and named the friendliest in his class.

Dad was elected sophomore vice president; he became a member of his class leadership council. A picture from an old yearbook shows him on a bench in the sun with his fellow class officers. He's wearing a white dress shirt, a tie, and glasses, and he's smiling so his upper teeth show. To Sydney Lou Hughes, he seemed perfect.

Although she barely cracked a book, Sydney Lou made good grades and was cast in every drama production on campus. The Elizabeth Taylor look-alike could act, too.

Excitement and promise filled the courtship. Mom fell in love with a man who she hoped would make her laugh and feel safe. Soon Sydney and Dad were holding hands and smiling as they walked the neat cement paths and hallways of the gray stone buildings at Phillips.

Dad's parents lived in Ponca City, Oklahoma, about twenty-five miles south of the Kansas border. His father was a military veteran and was the manager of a paint store. His mom was a stay-at-home mom and school secretary. They owned a small home and attended a local Disciples of Christ First Christian Church. In high school, Dad wrestled and played football. During hot summer days on the practice field, temperatures soared into the hundreds.

When Sydney Lou met Dad's parents for the first time during a visit to Ponca City, the four of them attended church together. Much like the congregation Mom had grown up in, the members of Dad's home church were all white. Shortly after that first visit, Dad proposed.

But he had to go to Claycomo, Missouri, to meet Mom's parents first. She grew up in the northeastern outskirts of Kansas City where Whitey and Pauline, by then, owned a used furniture store. The store sat opposite the family home on a seven-acre farm. Across the highway, a Ford assembly plant drove the Claycomo economy. Grandma and Grandpa owned the farm, the store, and the house. In the wake of World War II, other homes popped up nearby, but Grandma and Grandpa's place became a local landmark.

Grandpa Hughes built a barn behind the house, where Grandma raised horses and chickens. After the Great Depression, Grandpa refused to deposit money in a bank. He stashed cash around the farm instead. When he could, he traded furniture for goods and favors. His favorite currency was all about making a deal, even better when he helped out the other person.

Grandma Hughes was a steadfast believer. During her free time, she often sat at the family's dining room table, a thick slab of maple, and wrote sermons she gave to a local pastor. More than anything, Grandma wanted her daughter to marry a preacher, and she was thrilled when Sydney brought Dad home from college. When he asked for their daughter's hand in marriage, Whitey and Pauline gladly said yes.

To hear Mom tell it, the wedding was perfect. The ceremony took place at Liberty Christian Church, an old landmark built of red brick and limestone. A trio of stained-glass windows filled the sanctuary and showered more than two hundred attendees in multicolored light. Mom carried a bouquet of white roses down the aisle in a white dress with a short train. She and Dad knew fewer than half the guests. Though the wedding celebrated his daughter and new son-in-law, it gave Grandpa a chance to strengthen his business. If you knew Whitey Hughes back then, you probably made the guest list.

A few days after their wedding, Mom and Dad drove to Wichita and spent the summer working as youth counselors. When they returned to school, they moved into married-student housing. In 1957 Dad finished seminary and Mom completed her first year teaching high school. They also learned that Mom was pregnant.

I was born in Saint Mary's Hospital on October 11, 1957, less than two miles from Phillips University. Dad brought Mom flowers, and the two of them talked about how having a baby changed everything.

The following June, we moved to the parsonage in Edwardsville. During this time, Mom kept a journal about our lives together and about my growing up. Reading through it years later, I got the sense that she and Dad were happy. Mom wrote about how I slept in a century-old cradle passed through the family, about trips we took to a nearby park, and about how I first said "Daddy" when I was nine months old. Our lives revolved around the church calendar, and Dad quickly became one of Edwardsville's most respected citizens.

Not long after my second birthday, my life nearly ended when I was very ill. When Mom measured my temperature at 104 degrees, she filled the bathtub with ice water and lifted me inside. When the fever persisted, she called a doctor to the house. He prescribed penicillin and told my parents to get me to the hospital immediately. Further tests confirmed the doctor's diagnosis of spinal meningitis. The recommended cure was antibiotics for the short term and sunshine for a full recovery.

That spring, Mom and Grandma Hughes flew with me to Arizona. It was March, and snow covered the ground as we left Kansas. I remember my mom and Grandma Pauline putting me on a plane with them to Tucson, Arizona, for healthy sunshine. My mom and grandmom got sick on the bumpy ride, so without them noticing, I left my seat, slipped away, and went down the aisle to the front of the plane to make an announcement.

"Ladies and gentleman, I want everyone to meet my mom and grandma," I said, as they were cowering over a sick bag in their seats.

The streets of Tucson were just what the doctor ordered. I escaped again with my six shooters on both sides when I joined a staged bank robbery already in progress. I was promptly shot by the sheriff and dutifully fell over in the dust and was taken to jail. Afterward, the sheriff brought me an ice cream cone as a reward for such a fine performance before I was returned to my mother for safekeeping.

We stayed near Tucson for eighteen days. Mom wrote to Dad often. Years later, I found one of those letters inside her old journal.

It was written in blue pen and filled two sheets of what appeared to be motel stationary. Mom's handwriting, small and neat, had faded only slightly through the years:

> *Dearest One,*
>
> *We spent the entire day in the sun, and Scottie has a nice sunburn on his face and a slight pink on his arms. We still have the rented car so we drove out to "Old Tucson." They staged a robbery and capture by the Marshall when we first got there & Scottie went wild. He is like a bird just out of a cage. He has run until he could run no more . . . and eaten like a horse. I love you very very much & miss you terribly, but I'm convinced Scottie will be a big healthy new boy with a little of this medicine.*
>
> *How is snow? I hope it's gone so our meeting will be a wonderful success. I will be praying for its success. I love you so very much.*
>
> *Good night, sweetheart. All my love,*
> *Sydney*

I recovered completely from my illness. In July that year, our family drove to Texas and Mexico for a two-week vacation. We camped along the way. Mom's journal recalls boat rides, deep-sea fishing, and water skiing. Grandma and Grandpa Hughes joined us with Ricky and Patty, who were both a little older than me, and we became quick friends. A small black-and-white photo taken during that trip shows Ricky and me sitting on the tailgate of the Nash station wagon. Luggage and a giant tarp cover the roof of the car. We're both wearing white T-shirts, shorts, and big straw hats with "Mexico" written on the brims.

Later that year, Mom took me on a much shorter trip. Outside the Kansas City airport, she held me in her arms as Richard Nixon and his wife, Pat, arrived for a presidential campaign stop. As they walked past, Pat Nixon plucked a rose from a huge bouquet and handed it to me. That November, Richard Nixon lost to John F. Kennedy.

Scott and Ricky camping in Mexico

I remember another day from around this time, when Mom and I spent hours preparing a roast for dinner. I remember feeling excited about Dad coming home. The smell of meat, vegetables, and potatoes filled the parsonage. Shortly after Dad arrived, he began yelling when he noticed the cans of food in the kitchen cabinet were out of order.

"You can't even keep the cabinets neat," he said nastily.

"Well, I've made you dinner," Mom replied.

"Yeah, well, you can't even keep this kitchen clean. We need to clean up this mess."

"You can clean it up, but we're going to eat."

Dad threw one of the cans down and screamed, "I'm not going to eat until I get this cleaned up!"

Mom proceeded to empty the entire cabinet onto the floor. "Go to hell!" she yelled. She threw the silverware drawer at him and tried to run past.

Dad pushed Mom across the room and began to shake her. As Mom fought back, screams filled the house. I began to cry uncontrollably.

Dad's strength and weight overpowered Mom easily. Chaos filled the house. I had been setting our tiny card table with silverware.

I said, "Stop it. Stop it!" I covered my ears with my hands to try to drown out the noise. I still had a fork in my left hand. The next thing I knew, I was banging the large carving fork against an upright piano in the living room. Ivory shards flew from the piano keys with each clang of the fork. Suddenly, Mom ran through the living room. Dad chased her. His rage bulged from his neck and temples in thick veins of hate. Mom slammed shut the bathroom door. Dad pounded on it with both fists.

When Dad finally returned to the kitchen, he looked at me and said, "Don't worry yourself about it. Your mom just got upset with me, and now I have to clean it up. Go to your room." He knelt down and began to pick up the cans and silverware.

We never did eat the dinner Mom had so lovingly prepared. For the rest of our lives together, the broken piano keys reminded me of that night and when the façade of our happy home life abruptly ended.

Dad began to hit Mom regularly. I often woke to the sounds of his abuse. Closed in my room, I trembled in fear. In that tiny house, everything seemed so close, as if Dad were reaching through the darkness and hitting me, too.

I remember only two nursery rhymes: "The little boy who lived down the drain," not lane, and "inkin, blinkin, and nod," as I called it. I didn't have much of a childhood, and I had to grow up fast. But my mom would sing those songs to me when I was upset. The happy times from my boyhood consisted of my mother and me and the parallel lives we lived—imaginary and real. The sad times involved my mother and father, which invariably resulted in something awful and inexplicable.

I created imaginary friends. I was an only child with a vivid imagination, and they gave me a way to escape into a different world. I would never eat peas because they were my friends. I did my best to keep them safe from the flood waters caused when the gravy broke through the dam held up by mashed potatoes. There was also Mrs. Wrighley, my grown-up imaginary friend. We always set a place for her at the table and would never leave in the car until she had joined us.

One day, my mom stopped after going a short distance down the road and said, "Oh, we forgot Mrs. Wrighley!"

I responded, "It's okay, Mom. I shot her and she is now dead."

Imagination was critical to my survival. I could imagine a happy home, friends, and loved ones. The most important way Mom and I endured our situation was that she kept our lives focused on others and the world around us in a way that crowded out an unhappy and violent home. We could be happy outside.

In 1963, instead of starting kindergarten like most kids my age, I began first grade. That same fall, Mom started teaching at Bonner Springs High School, four miles west of Edwardsville. She had decided to begin teaching to help pay for a horse that she loved. Built in 1918, the old high school that felt enormous to me as a child still stands at the corner of Third and Cedar Streets. It looks like many public institutions in the area with a red brick façade on a limestone foundation.

More than three thousand people lived in town, many of them Black, and it was during the height of desegregation. Mom's classroom was in the school basement, and it was her first experience interacting with African Americans.

She taught special education and English, and her classes included almost every Black student on campus. She immersed herself in their lives and counseled students eagerly. Before long, rumors circulated about the pastor's wife and her fondness for Black students.

Mom picked me up from school every afternoon. Rather than going home, we often set out on counseling excursions. During one of these trips, I followed Mom through a cinder block house without electricity. Kerosene lanterns threw flickering light across dirt floors in the pitch dark. Six children lived inside and shared a single bed. There were three or four beds in one bedroom, all crammed together. The youngest, a baby, screamed when we arrived. I looked into the crib and saw that the child's hair was all gone. The older kids also had bald spots, where their skin had turned white.

Mom lifted the child close and patted its back until it quieted. As she did, I looked toward a dim corner of the room. Lots of little eyes stared back at me. The high-pitched squeal of rats sent chills through my body. Looking up, I saw blood seeping from the baby's scalp. On the way home, Mom told me the rats had eaten the child's hair.

Many of the Black families in eastern Kansas descended from tenant farmers, who had descended from slaves. Although Kansas was never a slave state, it played a dominant role in events leading up to the Civil War. Following the Kansas-Nebraska Act of 1854, pro- and anti-slavery supporters rushed into Kansas in hopes of influencing its stance on slavery. On January 29, 1861, Kansas entered the Union as a free state. Less than three months later, the Civil War began.

Despite its anti-slavery history, the Kansas community of my youth nourished racial prejudice. It seemed as if there was only one exception to this, and it was Sydney Lou. Mom never cared where people came from or how they looked. She only cared about helping them.

I remember one student in particular from her first year at Bonner Springs High. His name was Silas, and he was Black. Silas was the son of a single mother, and they lived above the tavern that she operated. He was gregarious and well known at school and around Bonner Springs. The year Silas left Bonner Springs High, the local newspaper ran photos of every graduating senior and a short description of their post-high school plans. Under Silas' name it reads: "My future plans are attending Phillips University in Enid, Oklahoma. I plan to major in Social Studies."

Silas was one of many Black students Mom led to Phillips. Grandpa Hughes helped by offering small scholarships. The application process was simple: Mom told Grandpa about the students, and Grandpa agreed to help pay their way. During Mom's own time at Phillips, she had watched proudly as the university enrolled its first two Black students. School segregation was ending throughout the South, and Mom and Dad had a front-row seat to the change.

School integration also affected me. In Edwardsville, I was one of the few white students to attend an interracial elementary school with Black and white students. As I moved through first grade, Mom often talked about the importance of treating all people equally. Dad delivered sermons on similar topics and wrote a column about family, religion, and sometimes race for the local newspaper. From the front pew of Edwardsville Christian Church, Mom and I listened carefully as he spoke.

Mom and I also began to escape across the Kansas River more and more to see Grandma and Grandpa Hughes. We spent most Saturdays with them in Claycomo. Grandma and Grandpa's farm became our refuge from home. On the same acreage where Mom grew up, I ran free. Ricky and Patty became my best friends. Ricky and Patty were two of the children who were left for dead by their parents. When my grandparents were asked to come and see these children, their heads were full of lice and they cried from hunger. Whitey and Pauline took Ricky and Patty, the youngest two, home with them. The older children were taken by other members of the community.

"Do you want to go to Grandma and Grandpa's house?" were my favorite words to hear.

It was about an hour from Bonner Springs, Kansas, to Claycomo, Missouri. But this was a safe haven. We rode horses, jumped on a giant trampoline, and made huge forts from hay bales in the barn. We'd play for hours until Grandma called us for dinner. On the best days, she served hamburgers, shakes, and fries from a nearby burger joint.

My grandparents knew about the abuse. The first time my dad hit my mom she was sitting on a toilet seat, eight months pregnant with me. He smacked her so hard that he knocked her off the seat. She told both sets of parents at the time, and they had a conversation with Dad. But they also asked Mom what she had done to provoke him. So while the farm was a sanctuary for us, my grandparents ignored the real reason we were there so often. It was never discussed.

CHAPTER TWO

Take Me with You

During the summer of 1964 racial tensions erupted in America. That July, President Lyndon Johnson signed the Civil Rights Act. Less than a year earlier JFK was assassinated. In Claycomo, I watched the president's funeral on my grandparent's color television. Soon afterward Dad supported efforts to form a local interracial ministerial alliance. One of the group's other members preached at Gethsemane Baptist, a Black church just two miles from our own.

Mom, Dad, and I visited Gethsemane together. When we arrived, the Reverend Jefferson Jackson stood outside. Jefferson and my dad were the first two co-chairs of the Black and White Ministerial Alliance. His small church was plastered in white stucco, and a white brick extension was under construction. The buildings rose from an otherwise empty field north of town. In the morning light, a white cross cast a long black shadow westward across the surrounding grass. Some of the church elders also stood outside. Like the Reverend, they wore dark suits, pressed white shirts, and thin dark ties.

Jefferson Jackson introduced the group with a firm handshake and a wide smile. He gave us a tour of the church grounds and the new construction that was being completed by church volunteers, cinder block by cinder block, and he led us inside to the front pew. Behind us, the rows of the sanctuary began to fill quickly. Almost all the men wore suits. The women wore long dresses, gloves, and hats. Mom recognized some of her students from school.

Gethsemane Church in 2012

Pastor Jefferson Jackson

Soon the building seemed to bulge. I couldn't believe how many people fit inside. My biggest surprise was yet to come. In a storm of energy and music, the choir exploded from behind a red curtain near the pulpit. Its members clapped and sang in unison as the congregation burst into song. Then, one by one, the elders stepped out. Music filled my body. Goose bumps spread across my arms. Suddenly, at a perfect crescendo of energy, the Reverend Jackson appeared in front of the church.

"Sing it, everyone!" he shouted.

The building pulsed. The reverend's voice carried with more grace and beauty than I had ever heard. His deep baritone sent vibrations through my body. I stood up, stunned. The man in front of me was a preacher unlike any I'd ever seen. He exuded electricity you could feel. That morning's service had the spark and flash of a lightning strike.

Jefferson Jackson was a handsome man of not quite six feet. He had loosely curled hair and a muscular frame built through years of manual labor. His smile was as broad as the Kansas River and just as easy. Jefferson was born in Bristow, Oklahoma, in the spring of 1922. His twin sister died at birth. All told, Jefferson's parents raised eight children—five boys and three girls.

Jefferson's dad was the son of a sharecropper and the first member of his family to own land. Jefferson grew up in a two-room house without running water or electricity. The girls slept in one bed and the boys in another. Family meals often included biscuits, bean lard, and grits. Jefferson would later recall how special those few times were each year when his mom put meat on the table.

Jefferson went barefoot for much of his childhood. Each afternoon after school, he worked in the fields with his siblings. By fourth grade, he nearly dropped out of school. His teacher convinced him to stay by giving him his first pair of shoes, and Jefferson managed to remain in school through tenth grade. He was later drafted into World War II. That same night, he fell to his knees and prayed. If God didn't send him to war, Jefferson promised to dedicate his life to serving the church.

Jefferson served in the military but was spared from being deployed overseas. Following his time in the service, he struggled to find work in Kansas City. Young, undereducated, and poor, he thought back on the day he was drafted. On a starry night, Jefferson walked outside alone and looked up.

"If you want me to serve you, send me a sign," he said. "Rattle the heavens!"

At that exact moment, a single shooting star left a fiery trail across the night sky.

Jefferson never looked back. He joined a gospel quartet and began taking ministry classes. He struggled to read and write, but he could read the Bible cover to cover. He paid his bills by working in the vast stockyards of Kansas City. Later, he picked up a warehouse job working nights. Along the way, he married a spirited woman everyone called Lulu. She loved outrageous hats almost as much as she loved sleeping around. Despite the cheating, Jefferson stayed. Lulu loved Jefferson for one reason: Their marriage made her the first lady at Gethsemane Baptist.

During our second visit to Gethsemane, Mom and I sat next to Lulu. Through the ministerial alliance, Jefferson had invited Dad to preach. That Sunday, Dad told a story from the book of Matthew. In it, a frenzied crowd surrounds Jesus as he heals two blind men. Dad used the story to talk about forgiveness and new life. It was a beautiful message . . . but it wasn't real. When his sermon ended, I looked at Mom. Tears poured from her eyes.

Mom's work helping Black students took a dramatic turn during my second year of school when she began mentoring Michael, a freshman in her last class of the day. One of six children, Michael lived in the Black section of Bonner Springs. He was fourteen years old and one of the smallest freshmen in his class. After school, Michael often lingered in Mom's classroom. He'd sit quietly reading or doing homework. Eventually Mom offered him a ride home. When they arrived at his house, Mom saw Michael's dad unconscious in the dirt yard. Stepping over him, she followed Michael inside, met his mom, and left.

Back at school, Michael began to confide in Mom about his family. Sitting in her classroom long after the final bell, he painted a dismal picture of life at home. His dad was perpetually drunk and usually violent. His mom seemed forever detached, like the walking dead. Mom felt deeply troubled by the stories Michael shared with her and desperately wanted to protect him from this disturbing environment.

Eventually, Mom and I drove together to Michael's house. As we pulled up, I saw him sitting on the front step. He smiled as we walked toward him.

"Sydney, what are you doing here?" Michael asked.

"I'm here to take you home with us, where you'll be safe," Mom replied.

As we spoke, his mother appeared on the porch. Mom told her matter-of-factly that Michael was coming to live with us.

Michael's mom stared at her blankly and said, "Go on, Michael, go with them." She nodded and walked back inside. Michael never would have survived in that house. He was far too different from his tough siblings, who ultimately wound up in jail.

At the parsonage, we set up a cot in the laundry room. Michael became so used to the sound of the washer and dryer that he preferred to sleep with them running. They also muffled the sounds of Dad's abuse. Michael never upset Dad—he did his chores and never talked back. When Dad hit Mom, Michael disappeared silently.

Scott's "brother" Michael

I looked up to Michael from the start. He was twice my age, and he dressed with a flare otherwise unseen in Edwardsville. I grew to love Michael as my brother. He helped me feel safe when our house turned violent. He would try to distract me during a fight, taking me on excursions in the car. We would flee to the grocery store or the high school, or our favorite escape—shopping for clothes.

By 1966 Dad's abuse was no longer a family secret. While most of my mom's bruises weren't outwardly visible, elders in the church became aware of the situation because she often sought protection in other houses down the street. At Edwardsville Christian, rumors about Mom and her students also spread. That spring, after almost eight years, Dad lost his pastorship. While he searched for a new position, Dad, Mom, Michael, and I stayed with Grandma and Grandpa Hughes. We joined Dad for a couple of family job interviews. On one Sunday, he delivered a guest sermon at a large church in an affluent area of Kansas City. Michael joined us near the front of the all-white congregation. We were never asked to return.

Dad eventually took over as director of Tall Oaks, a Christian camp and conference center west of Bonner Springs. It occupied a few hundred acres along the north bank of the Kansas River. The day we moved in, I fell in love with the place. Huge oak trees shaded the property and turned a rusty orange each fall. Scattered throughout, broad meadows and bunkhouses welcomed visitors year-round, especially in summer. A single-lane gravel road meandered through the grounds, passing the dining hall, cabins, a pool with two diving boards, and a large open-air A-frame shelter that served as a chapel. At the end of the road, a rugged bluff grew thick with oak trees and angled steeply toward the river.

The camp director's house felt like a mansion compared to the parsonage. With a family room, a formal living room, large kitchen, three bedrooms, two bathrooms, a double-car garage, and a basement, it made the parsonage look like a cage. For the first time in his life, Michael had his own bedroom.

At Tall Oaks, I often walked through the woods alone and explored the places few campers ever saw. I hiked game trails and made a few of my own. But my favorite activity was sitting in the midst of the oak trees, high on the bluff, and looking south over the railroad tracks and river. Sandbars and deep green thickets dotted the river's course. During fall and winter, after the leaves fell, you could see the water pass slowly below and watch trains roll west toward Lawrence or east toward the small town of De Soto and beyond there to Bonner Springs and Edwardsville. At the top of the bluff, the trains sounded soft and faint, not at all like they had for so many years when living right next to the tracks.

About the time we moved to Tall Oaks, Mom bought thirty-five acres on the outskirts of Edwardsville. Grandma and Grandpa lent her the money and helped us build a small barn with a tack house. Shortly afterward, Grandpa drove us across the river to an Arabian horse farm in De Soto. I fell in love with a black colt named Midnight. Grandpa bought him for me, and we eventually kept four horses on the property.

Back at Tall Oaks, we quickly established a family routine. Each morning Mom and Michael drove to Bonner Springs while Dad and I ate breakfast. Mom continued to teach at the high school, and Michael became heavily involved with school activities. He acted in plays, made the honor roll, and led the band as drum major. As a senior, he was pictured on eight pages of the school yearbook, more than almost anyone else.

While Michael flourished, my relationship with my father disintegrated. In Edwardsville, Dad and I had rarely spent time alone. Now, each morning over cereal and toast, the barrier between us was stripped raw. The gaps in our relationship became chasms. I wasn't interested in anything he did, and he cared little about me. I think Dad saw me as an adversary rather than a son. During the long silences that hung over breakfast, I felt anger toward my father. I was angry with him for what he was and for what he wasn't, for what he did to my mom and for what he failed to do with me.

"Scottie, are you ready for school?" Dad asked one morning.

"Of course I'm ready for school!" I responded sullenly.

"Well, wash your dishes," he said. Everything always had to be perfectly in order.

"I *always* wash my dish," I replied with a bit of attitude.

"Don't you know not to talk like that to your father?" Dad shouted through gritted teeth.

Inevitably, something I said always struck him the wrong way. I hated those moments.

After breakfast, Dad drove me two miles to Linwood Elementary School. Fewer than five hundred people lived in town. If nothing else, Linwood was poor. A small post office accounted for most of the town activity. When Dad didn't drive me to school, I caught the bus at the end of the camp road or drove in with Slim, the camp handyman. Slim was white, skinny, and tall. I remember his presence standing in stark contrast to Dad, who by then weighed much more than he did during his college years. Slim obeyed Dad without question and quickly became his most trusted employee.

On Sundays, our family attended church a few blocks from the University of Kansas in Lawrence. Afterward, we returned straight home. Dad worked in his office and Mom read the newspaper in the living room. While Michael caught up on homework, I played war with little pretend plastic soldiers made of dominoes and Lincoln Logs. I would often stop playing and check on my mom to make sure she was okay.

On one of these Sundays, I went to check on Mom. I was watching from the next room when Dad approached her from behind. He lifted his hands and began to rub her shoulders. Then he curled his fingers around her throat and began to squeeze. I froze. I could see Mom convulse and the color drain from her face. From my hiding spot in the next room, I watched in what seemed like slow motion as Mom coughed and grabbed her throat in desperation. Then, just as quickly as it had begun, Dad released his grip and walked away.

Each night as I fell asleep, I wondered if he'd hit her before morning. My nightmares became reality. I'd wake to the sound of screaming or of Dad pounding on the bathroom door. On the worst nights, I could hear Dad hitting her, followed by whimpers of pain and tears. Through it all, Mom kept working, even when I woke to the sound of the front door slamming and gravel crunching in the driveway, as she sped away into the night.

I once tried to stop Dad from hurting Mom. I was in bed when the noise began. When I heard the bathroom door slam, I got up. Dad turned in the hallway to find me staring at him.

"Go back to your room," he said, looking down at me. "Your mother locked herself in the bathroom again. I can't stop her. All I want to do is stop her from hurting herself. She's crazy. You know that."

I could hear Mom crying on the other side of the door. I spoke in my loudest voice.

"Mom, are you okay? Can you come out? Can you tell me you're okay?"

The bathroom door swung open and Mom rushed out wearing her nightgown.

"I'm okay," she said. "Go back to bed. He won't hurt you."

She ran down the hall, grabbed her keys and purse, and started for the front door. Dad tried to follow her, but I stepped in front of him. He stopped. It was all the time Mom needed.

My greatest fear as a child was that my mom would leave and not take me with her—those nights when she would run past, barefoot out the door, I would put my head through the curtains against the window to see her drive off in her Volkswagen bug, knowing she was finally safe that night. She would reappear early the next morning in time to get ready for school and drive away again to escape to the safety of the classroom and work. But I feared that one day she would not return . . . and I would be left behind.

By night, my mom was a tortured and battered housewife. By day, Sydney Lou was a high school English teacher for special needs students, a pastor's wife, and a community activist. She was also a faithful friend, an accomplished piano player, and a creative artist. Sydney Lou showed Tennessee walking horses, mentored troubled kids, produced church plays and pageants, made murals for the school and church, and spent long hours consoling friends in need. Whether doing this was to get away or to express compassion to others and feel self-worth, she would go and I would accompany her. Sometimes, we just went to a movie or drove to Grandpa and Grandma's house—the ultimate retreat. When Mom said, "Do you want to go with me?" I would always reply with great conviction, "Take me with you," and I was out the door and in the passenger seat of the Volkswagen before she could change her mind.

There are only a few days from around this time that I look back on fondly, mainly the days when Mom and I played hooky from school. Without Dad knowing, one hot day in late spring we took off toward Edwardsville, turned north across the railroad tracks, and drove along a series of one-lane roads. On the way, we saw livestock and tiny homes on tiny farms. Many of the buildings were in disrepair. We turned down a dirt road, drove past a rundown house, and stopped in front of a pigpen and a large chicken coop. Looking around, I saw an old emerald green Ford truck. Nearby, a Black man wearing overalls and a straw hat walked toward us.

The first feature I recognized about the Reverend Jefferson Jackson was his smile. Mom explained that she and Jefferson had become friends since our visits to Gethsemane Baptist, as Jefferson showed us around the small plot of land he had rented where he could grow some vegetables, have a chicken coop, and keep his pigs. While we strolled around the property, he spoke about how he had raised animals and worked on a farm since he was a kid. I remember the smell of pigs rolling in the mud.

"Here, take this bucket and try to get it over the fence," Jefferson said, including me as he fed the pigs. "Take this cabbage."

"Jefferson, this pig is going to eat my hand!" I yelled in delight.

"Boy, that pig's not going to eat your hand," he laughed good-naturedly.

After a while, the three of us jumped into Jefferson's green truck. We drove along more dirt roads and eventually parked by a large pond, behind a line of cars. For the rest of the day, I caught more carp than I could count. Jefferson taught me how to roll giant stinky globs of cornmeal into bait balls and make them stick to the hook. There must have been thousands of fish in that pond. Wherever I looked, people were reeling them in. Along the entire shore, Mom and I were the only white people.

The places we would go to escape weren't always so secret. Mom's passion and commitment to her beloved horse "Lady in Silver" was one such diversion. She had spent a good portion of her meager teacher's salary, $10,000, to buy Lady in Silver, a pure white Tennessee Walking Horse for show. Lady in Silver was trained and boarded outside of Kansas City. One summer, we drove the long distance four days a week so that Mom could train and ride Lady in Silver. Every weekend, we met the trainer and the horse at a competition or show. Mom was amazing to watch on that horse. She would dye her hair at the beauty parlor a different color every week to match her outfit—red, lavender, pink, black, and silver. The two of them would then light up the show ring with a sea of sequins. The kids at school always wondered what color hair she would have each week. After fourteen 1st place ribbons, Mom and Lady in Silver entered and won 4th place in the American Royal. Her hair fell out at the end of the show season from all that bleaching, but it was glorious while it lasted. We would both have a passion for horses for many years to come.

Sydney Lou with Lady in Silver

In April 1968 I was ten years old. I didn't know much about Martin Luther King Jr. I knew he was a civil rights leader, and I knew he was a pastor. That second part resonated most with me. When I heard the news about King's assassination, I remember thinking how Dad and King had something in common. I also thought about Jefferson. I wondered if other Black pastors would be shot.

Mom had been at school when it happened. She still taught most of the Black students in the high school, either in her special education or regular English classes. After the news spread, the principal announced over the loud speaker that all the Negro students could go home for the day. Mom immediately rushed out of her classroom to the administrative office to protest. She believed the high school was giving the wrong message by treating the white students different from the Black students. Sending only the Black students home could cause even more of a racial divide and social unrest, she argued. The principal finally agreed with Mom, and all students were then given the option to leave school for the rest of the day.

Less than twenty-four hours after King's shooting, hundreds of high school and college students marched in downtown Kansas City. City officials assigned every Black officer they had to help control the crowd. For a week, Mom and Dad read the newspaper anxiously. People all around the country feared riots. At home, we watched television broadcasts of the violence in Chicago and Washington, DC. Towns across the rest of America grew restive. But many remained calm, including ours.

Two months after King's assassination, one early spring day, Mom unexpectedly picked me up from school. Linwood was a lot closer to Tall Oaks where we lived and my dad worked. Mom commuted each day some thirty miles on her trip back and forth Bonner Springs High School, so it was a big surprise when she arrived to take me home.

"I have something to tell you, and I needed you to hear it from me," she said, as we drove home in the car. "Dad and I are getting a divorce. I have told him I don't want anything from him—except you. You can still visit your dad but you will live with me. We will be moving as soon as the school year is over, back to Edwardsville. We will live on the farm property there. So I need to know," she said, "are you okay with all this?"

At first, I didn't know what to say. Thoughts and questions as jumbled as a sunflower field after the harvest flooded my brain. Then a sense of relief and joy overcame me. No longer would I live in fear. I began to rattle off questions.

"What did he say to you when you told him you were leaving?" I asked.

"Well, he wasn't happy about it, but he also wasn't sad because I think he wanted to get rid of me."

"What about me? Did he want me, too?" I asked.

That last question stuck. We had been driving aimlessly around Linwood. Mom pulled over, stopped the car, and looked at me. "More important," she said, "is that I want you. I told him that I would not take any money from him if I could have full custody and take you. And he said fine."

"What about furniture?"

"We'll take Grandpa's furniture."

"Where will we live?"

"We'll get a mobile home and put it on the farm. If you don't want to go, I understand."

"Well, you're not gonna leave me, are you?" I asked desperately.

"No, of course not," Mom replied.

"You have to take me with you. You can't leave me. You have to take me with you," I pleaded.

Michael left for Phillips University that summer. Grandpa Hughes paid his way. Not long after he moved out, we'd gone to the farm to check on the animals, and Michael told Mom he needed to speak to her. They sat in the car until it grew dark and talked for a long time while I waited outside.

"Sydney, I have something I have to tell you," he said. "I have feelings for other men."

"Why did you want to tell me?" Mom asked.

"Because," he said, "I knew you'd still love me."

Michael was a talented young man who was ostracized from his family and from his peers in school. He would eventually die of HIV AIDS before there was a known treatment. We kept in touch and visited over the years, and even had dinner with Michael and his partner. But we had no idea how sick he was.

Mom and I moved to the farm near Edwardsville. She bought a doublewide aluminum trailer that was white with a silver roof and parked it next to the barn. Mom transformed the tack room of the barn into our living room, which was now conveniently attached to the trailer to expand our humble living space. Grandma and Grandpa Hughes provided fancy new furniture that rested on the dark turquoise indoor/outdoor carpeting covering the concrete slab. We embraced our new lives on the farm and used our acreage to grow a variety of vegetables and raise animals, who often wound up eating the tomatoes, lettuce, radishes, and squash.

Along with our horses, we kept seven pigs and a goat. One of our pigs had a hole in his side, with a colostomy bag hanging down. We also had four cats, two dogs, and a guinea pig. My dog Dewey had passed away by then; someone had poisoned him. On hot days, the horses shaded themselves under large persimmon trees that grew near

Sydney feeding her pet pig

the fence line. During long summer nights, sunsets turned the farm golden while warm winds blew across the sloping fields.

To my chagrin, Mom made sure we brought the piano with the chipped ivory keys with us and placed it prominently in the living room. For as long as I can remember, my mother made me take piano lessons. At first I wanted to, but then it was always time for me to come inside to practice the piano while the other kids got to stay outside and play. I never played very well. I had enough of an ear for it, but I didn't put the time into learning how to read music easily. After we moved into the trailer on the farm, Mom made me start piano lessons again. In the summer months the tack room with the concrete floor underneath remained cool. But in the winter, it was cold and there was no way to get warm with just the electric portable wall heater. Nonetheless, I would bundle up and try to concentrate enough to at least pretend to be practicing.

One day after school while pretending to practice, I started to think about Mom and all she had sacrificed for me, and I wrote a song for her. It went something like this:

> *My mother used to sit me on her lap.*
> *She would read me the stories of the Bible.*
> *I would love to hear them so very much.*
>
> *Now I know, Lord, Now I know, Lord, that someday you'll come for me.*
>
> *When that Day comes, when that day comes, Lord, the angels will sing out in heaven, and the heavens will open for you and for me.*
>
> *On that day, Lord, my mother and I will be free.*

Shortly after leaving Tall Oaks, Mom and I became the first white members of Gethsemane Baptist. We also began to see much more of Jefferson. He often drove by the farm, and sometimes he and Mom sat outside until dusk. I watched them from inside the trailer. By fall of 1968, my parent's divorce became official. Soon afterward Jefferson spent the night, and he and Mom lived together unmarried.

I began fifth grade. I did well in school, which caused some jealousy among the other students. It was the early days of integration, and the majority of the students in our school were Black. One day at recess some of the Black boys began taunting me because they knew about Mom and Jefferson.

I had come out into the hall to wait in line for the water fountain. The bathroom nearby had two entrances—one from inside the hall and another that led outside to the playground, volleyball courts, and a large field. When I finished taking a drink, I entered the bathroom to head outside and a few of the boys stopped me.

"I know that your mom and Jefferson are together. Thanks a lot for ruining our church," one of them said.

"Boy, your mom sure did create a mess," said another one.

"Well, that's the way it goes," said the first boy. "These white women can't keep away from a Black stud."

"She didn't try to ruin your church," I argued. "You don't know what you're talking about!"

"Well, she was just looking for a Black stud."

"You better watch your mouth!"

"I don't need to watch my mouth. Your mom's a n-gger lover."

My fists reacted before my brain. I hit him and he hit back. I hit him again and then started to run, but both boys pulled me down on the ground in a tug of war.

A few minutes later, I sat in the principal's office. My lip was bleeding badly and tears streamed down my face. When I got home, I told Mom what had happened. She looked sad. Then she made sure my butt hurt, too. Fighting wasn't allowed—period.

"No matter what they say to you, you can't respond," she said. "You have to be bigger than that."

Dad also had issues with Mom dating Jefferson. He picked me up from the farm every other weekend, and he asked lots of questions about them, about what they did and if Jefferson spent the night. One time, Dad arrived and knocked on the door, wanting to come in, rather than leaving right away like we usually did.

"I just want to come in for a bit," he said.

"Why?" I asked.

"I just want to look around and see that you're safe."

"I'm safe," I replied as he began to walk into the bedrooms.

"Why are you in my mom's room?" I asked. He went into the bathroom and started counting the toothbrushes. "You're not supposed to do this," I continued.

"It looks like someone else is living here," he said.

"That's none of your business," I said angrily.

Once we arrived at Tall Oaks, I went straight to my bedroom.

Dad came in and said, "Maybe we'll go to a hockey game this weekend."

"That sounds good," I said. "I've never been to a hockey game."

"I want to talk to you about something first," Dad said seriously. "You and your mom are living with a Black man in sin. I want to get you out of this situation."

"I don't need to be out of it," I argued.

"Your mom has lots of issues and likes Black men," he kept on.

"You don't know what the hell you're talking about!" I yelled. "You beat her for years! I don't want to go anywhere with you. Get out. Get out!"

I insisted he take me home the next morning. It was the first time I realized he was humiliated by the situation. It wasn't about me or my safety; it was solely about the fact that it was embarrassing to him. Somewhere deep down I began to understand that he was going to cause trouble for me.

My visits with Dad almost always ended badly. He bad-mouthed Mom constantly. He said she had a *thing* for Black men. He accused her of visiting students at Phillips University and of cheating on him during their marriage.

He also spoke badly of Jefferson. "Do you really want to live with . . ." he'd pause, drawing out the final two words, "*Black people?*"

I never understood where Dad's hatred began. My dad's father told my mom that it was because my dad used to see him beat his own wife, my dad's mother. In Edwardsville, Dad worked hard to help the races find common ground. That's how we'd met Jefferson in the first place. He even wrote a regular newspaper column on religion, often covering race relations and the importance of breaking the color barriers that defined so many churches. Years later, no matter how hard I tried to give Dad the benefit of the doubt, I never could. He'd either been a racist in disguise all along or turned into one when Mom fell in love with Jefferson. Either way, his feelings ripped an even greater divide between us.

Less than a year after the divorce, Mom lost her job at Bonner Springs High. The principal told her she might be happier if she left. He didn't need to say anything else. By being together, Mom and Jefferson challenged people's accepted boundaries. They were the only mixed-race couple most people knew. When students and faculty began to gossip about the white teacher and the Black preacher, Mom's days at Bonner Springs High were done.

Jefferson also left Gethsemane Baptist. He kept his day job working in a warehouse for a sporting goods company in Kansas City. Not long after he and Mom began seeing each other, Jefferson gave me a basketball and nailed up a hoop at the farm. We often shot baskets together until it was too dark to see. That ball became my new best friend.

Jefferson had a mean hook shot and he would laugh and say, "Boy, you can't shoot." Then I would shoot and make a basket and get ahead of him, and we'd laugh. He never gritted his teeth or said a bad word about anyone, in contrast to my real dad, who always had something nasty to say. During these times, I realized that you could have happy moments, that there was such a thing as family. A man's role didn't have to revolve only around being the disciplinarian. You didn't have to fear a father figure.

Mom found a new job teaching high school equivalency courses in Kansas City. She also tried to get me to join an all-Black Boy Scout troop. During my first meeting, one of the older boys made me stand on my head against a wall the entire time. I never went back.

It took Jefferson's first wife almost two years to sign her divorce papers. Soon afterward, he and Mom spent a weekend in Nebraska. When they returned, they were married. It was still not accepted for an interracial couple to be married in Kansas. As a wedding gift, Jefferson gave Mom a white miniature poodle she named Trixie.

A few months after their marriage, the three of us took a day trip through the Kansas countryside. We spent hours driving through the hills and over long flat expanses, finding places none of us had seen before. It was a perfect day. When we returned home, we saw a narrow column of smoke rising near the farm. Jefferson skidded to a stop in front of our gate. Looking out the truck window, I saw a small wooden cross smoldering in a pile of ashes.

"What is it, a cross?" I asked.

Jefferson replied, "Boy, we don't know. Don't worry about it."

"Who would put something like that there? Why would they set a fire next to our driveway?"

Jefferson got out of the pickup to open the farm gate. When he got back to the car, he said, "Someone who just doesn't know any better. You just have to never mind people like that."

It was one more reminder that we were different and not accepted. It was interesting how quickly people thought the same thoughts about me and my mom that they thought about Jefferson because of his skin color. That burning cross was aimed at all three of us. I didn't escape it.

Dad filed for custody of me. In court, he claimed Mom wasn't fit to raise me. The judge made vague references to Mom's associations with "Black people" and called her out for marrying Jefferson, who he referred to as "a Negro."

One weekend around this time, Dad drove to Missouri to pick me up from my grandparents' house. Mom told me to hide in the attic with Ricky and Patty. We turned off the lights and tried not to make any noise. Dad came to the front door and knocked. When no one answered, he moved to the side door and knocked again. Then he yelled my name and pounded on the door. Upstairs, I pressed myself flat on the floor and breathed slowly. I knew Dad could break down the door easily. I heard him walk across the driveway back toward his car. As he sped away, I looked out the attic window and saw him circling the block. He parked in front of the furniture store and went inside. He found Mom and started yelling. Jefferson was there and told him to calm down. Grandpa pulled down a horsewhip from a wall and chased Dad off the property.

Dad's attorney called the next day. Two lawyers watched as Mom delivered me to Dad. At the end of the weekend, I went back to Mom. Soon I wouldn't have that choice.

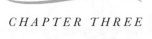

CHAPTER THREE

Leaving It All Behind

The night before my final custody decision, Mom and Jefferson drove me to Claycomo, Missouri. We had started the day in Lawrence, Kansas, where the court hearing was held. Earlier that day, the judge had refused to allow my testimony. Throughout the trial, he never asked me where I wanted to live, meaning with which parent. After the hearing, Mom and Jefferson met with our attorney, while I waited in the hall. More than an hour passed before they emerged. Mom's eyes were red.

In the parking lot, I sat between Mom and Jefferson on the bench seat of Jefferson's truck. As we drove away, Mom began to cry. Through her tears, I heard her say something.

"Scottie, we're going to lose you."

I was shocked. How could this be? I hadn't been allowed to tell the judge how scared I was of my dad, to tell him about all the abuse I had witnessed, about how Dad hit and choked Mom, about his anger, violence, and bigotry. Mom's worst news was yet to come.

"We might not get to see you at all," she said. "The judge doesn't think Jefferson and I should be married, and no one thinks you should be living with us, not even our own attorney. I'm sorry, Scottie. We tried."

I stared at the floor of the truck. Tears welled in my eyes. I didn't stop crying until I noticed Jefferson pass the turnoff to Edwardsville.

"We're going to Grandma and Grandpa's," Mom said.

When we arrived, Grandma gave me a huge hug. For dinner, Grandpa brought home my favorite milkshake, hamburgers, and fries. We ate and joked and laughed and tried not to think about what was coming. After we ate, we moved to the living room. Ricky and I sat together on a couch with overstuffed pillows. Across the room, Grandpa sat with the others and spoke quietly.

"You're going to lose tomorrow," he said. "If you don't show up, you'll be held in contempt. The only way to keep Scottie is to leave the country."

I couldn't believe what I was hearing. No one had said anything about this on the drive or during dinner. Looking across the room, I saw Grandpa's eyes. They looked sad.

"Then we'll just have to leave," Mom said. "We have no choice if we want to be together, and Jefferson and I can't leave Scottie behind."

Where would we go? Canada or Mexico seemed the most logical choices. Mom and I had been to Mexico before, but Jefferson had not. We all agreed that going south of the border for the three of us didn't make sense, because we knew there was just as much prejudice toward an interracial family there. We chose Canada. Mom had an aunt in Bremerton, Washington, near Vancouver, British Columbia, and Jefferson had a sister and family living outside of Seattle. We didn't know if we would be able to contact any of them. We would be on our own regardless of which country we sought refuge in. Grandpa Whitey would do what he could to help us, buying our tickets and giving us a wad of cash.

The rest of the night passed in a blur. We arrived back home very late and pulled out our suitcases. Jefferson went outside to feed the animals one last time. Mom told me to pack what I needed that could fit in one bag. I deflated my basketball as much as I could and packed it first. Next, I packed a set of dominos, some comic books, and a pair of drumsticks. In the little space that remained, I stuffed some clothes and a toothbrush and then fell asleep. Mom shook me awake before dawn. I could hear Jefferson down the hall. I took a quick shower, while he carried our suitcases out to the truck. Mom was the only one allowed to bring two bags. In her second, she packed Trixie. Just before we drove away, Jefferson handed me the key to the front door of the trailer.

"Go lock the door, Boy, and let's go," he said.

And we were gone.

Later that morning, as our flight lifted off, a judge's gavel fell in a half-empty courtroom. Somewhere beyond Kansas, I looked out a small oval window and watched the plains turn to rocky peaks, stabs of realization that we had, in the middle of a night that already seemed like a dream, packed our bags and run away. Behind us were the first twelve years of my life and the place I called home. We had left behind Dad, the evil lawyers, and a judge who wouldn't hear my story.

Hours later, looking out that same window, I saw only clouds. When they broke, snow-covered mountains filled the porthole. So did the tallest trees I had ever seen, sparkling water, and a city with sky-scrapers that seemingly rose from the sea. Vancouver, British Columbia, stretched out below.

Fewer than twenty-four hours had passed since Grandma unfolded a partially torn road map on the living room coffee table and Grandpa placed his finger on a large dot in the upper left-hand corner. He'd visited the Northwest once before.

"It's beautiful country," he said. Now I knew what he meant.

A few days after we arrived, Mom called Grandpa from a payphone.

"They held you in contempt," he told her. "There's a court order demanding your return. They're going to charge you with kidnapping."

Mom hung up. It was April 1970.

In Vancouver, it hadn't taken long for Mom and Jefferson to discover that finding work would be nearly impossible. During our first dinner in the city, they listened carefully as our waitress, an immigrant from Hong Kong, described the detailed paperwork required to obtain work permits. The more she talked, the more they realized how unprepared we were to run away. Any paperwork would be too much for a family trying to hide.

The ferry from mainland Canada to Vancouver Island carried hundreds of passengers and cars. We planned to cross to the island and reenter the US on another ferry. If all went well, we'd slip back into the country at a little-known border crossing in the western reaches of Washington State.

As our second ferry steered south, we had no idea what, or who, was waiting for us on the other side. During the nearly four-hour crossing, Mom filled out our customs' sheets. She used Jefferson's last name for all of us. We were taking a huge risk. If we'd somehow given ourselves away, we'd walk right into the hands of the police. If we hadn't, we had no plan. Only one thing was certain: The little money we had wouldn't last long.

"Get out the maps." Mom's voice snapped us to action. She suddenly looked very serious. In the days since we'd left Kansas, she had remained upbeat and excited. Now a wave of responsibility seemed to capsize her.

Seated near one of the ferry's huge windows, we spread various maps across a large table. We studied unfamiliar highway numbers and read the names of small towns printed next to tiny dots. As we did, whitecaps formed on the water outside and I began to daydream.

Mom and Jefferson were so engrossed in their maps that they didn't even notice the stranger approaching our table. He was tall and wore a plaid sport coat, dress slacks, and a felt hat with a feather on one side.

"Where are you folks headed?" he asked, startling Mom.

Her reply sounded on edge. "We're not sure."

"I couldn't help overhear your conversation," the stranger said. "It sounds like you're looking for a new place to live."

We should have asked his name or what he wanted. We were certainly the oddest-looking family aboard the ship. Mom was carrying Trixie in an oversized purse, I refused to let go of my half-deflated basketball, and Jefferson was the only Black man on board. When I considered how we looked, I began to realize most people actually seemed to be avoiding us. If any of us wondered why the stranger had approached, we never had time to ask.

"You might try Sequim," he said. "They'll accept you there. People from all over the world are relocating there."

Then he touched the brim of his feathered hat and walked away. We re-entered the US in Port Angeles, Washington, a small timber and fishing town on the northern edge of the Olympic Peninsula. Seattle was the nearest big city, three hours away. We passed through customs and immigration without incident and took a taxi, after a few disconcerting looks from the driver, to a nearby hotel. It overlooked a small strip of downtown businesses and a large harbor. A vacancy sign hung outside. In the lobby, the front-desk attendant looked at us and said they were full. Jefferson smiled, said thank you, and ushered us back outside. We walked silently past the vacancy sign. A hotel on the next block also advertised rooms. We opened the front door and went inside. This time, the attendant checked us in.

Later that evening we walked into the downtown area. Standing on the waterfront, we looked back toward Canada. A huge oil tanker moved silently along the Strait of Juan de Fuca, the same body of water we'd crossed earlier that day. On the other side, I could see the lights of Victoria, British Columbia. The smell of saltwater hung in the air.

The next morning we found a car dealership. Jefferson eyed a turquoise Studebaker sedan on the lot. He drove it around the block. When he returned, he took four hundred dollars from his wallet and bought the car. Our bags fit easily in the trunk. I sat in back, Mom carried Trixie in the passenger seat, and Jefferson drove.

Blue Mountain Road leaves US Highway 101 about midway between Port Angeles and Sequim, towns separated by fifteen miles of a one-lane highway. It was one of the more rural roads in an already rural part of western Washington. Shortly after leaving the highway, the road climbs steeply into the foothills of the Olympic Mountains. Large farms and old barns bracket the narrow road.

As Jefferson drove us up Blue Mountain for the first time, the Studebaker began to groan. The possibility of breaking down suddenly seemed very real. I thought, *what if the police show up to help? Will they find out who we were and send us back to Kansas? Are they following us already?*

As the Studebaker pushed forward, I considered the terrible consequences of failure. I distracted myself by spotting deer in nearby meadows as we passed. In some ways, the landscape wasn't so different from the outskirts of Edwardsville. In others, it was half a world away. At their far edges, the fields grew into thick forests. As we kept climbing, I began to feel certain about one thing: No one would find us up here.

It took half an hour to reach our destination. Earlier that morning, Jefferson had seen a job listed in a local newspaper for a ranch caretaker. When he called, the owner said to stop by.

As we neared the top of Blue Mountain Road, I saw a large house surrounded by broad meadows and dense stands of Douglas fir trees with white pole fences, marking the vast boundaries of the ranch. Dozens of deer grazed in the distance. Mr. Chapel, the man who had placed the caretaker ad, was expecting us. Jefferson turned up the driveway and parked. A barn and a small trailer stood nearby. As we opened the car doors, two dogs greeted us. Behind them, a tall rancher with wide shoulders, a large frame, and graying hair walked toward us from the house. A silver belt buckle from his waist shone in the sun, and he carried a cowboy hat in his left hand.

"You must be Jefferson," he said.

"Yes, sir. And you must be Mr. Chapel." Jefferson motioned toward Mom and me. "This is my wife, Sydney, and my number one son, Scottie."

Mr. Chapel took a long look at us. If he was surprised Jefferson was Black and Mom wasn't, he didn't show it.

"Nice to meet you folks," he said. He shook our hands and put on his hat. "Well, we better take a look around."

It was a large spread with open fields, trees, fences, ponds, and horses. As he showed us around, Mr. Chapel asked Jefferson about his experience with animals and land. He must have been satisfied with Jefferson's answers because he soon showed us the caretaker's residence. It was a trailer, smaller than our trailer back home, but at least there were two bedrooms.

"That's about all there is," Mr. Chapel said. "If you want, you can stay for a few days and see how you like the place."

Jefferson's smile was as big as I'd seen since before we left Kansas.

For the next few days, Mr. Chapel showed us how he liked things done. He kept his ranch in good working order and expected the same from us. The work wasn't hard. Jefferson mowed the meadows to just the right level for the deer, put out salt licks, and kept oats in the troughs for the horses. Mom fed the dogs and looked after the big house when Mr. Chapel was away. I fed the fish in two ponds. For that, Mr. Chapel paid us room and board.

Admittedly, my job was the easiest. Sometimes, tossing food into the ponds, I thought about the day Mom, Jefferson, and I went fishing outside Edwardsville. It was one of the happiest days I could remember. As I daydreamed atop Blue Mountain Road, I thought about Dad.

I can't tell people much about him. He never, or almost never, touched or abused me directly. But it was the fear of his temper escalating out of control—the sense that anything could displease him at any time—that kept me on guard as a child. He was large, even obese. I never wanted to look like him. It didn't help when so many people said "you look just like your father." He was a man of the cloth, but we never prayed or sang or had joy at home. There were a few okay memories in spite of his terrible abuse of my mother. Those days before school, he would make me breakfast after my mom had left to teach school; these were tolerable times if I didn't spill anything or question how the eggs were cooked or ask too many questions.

There were the rare occasions when he would wrestle or, better yet, play basketball with me. Most of the time, I played basketball by myself, pretending to be both teams. As an only child, I learned how to use my imagination for almost everything. What I didn't understand so outweighed what I did. I never understood why he hit my mom. I never understood why he kept a diary about how crazy Mom was, and I never understood why a local hairdresser from church was always at our house with her husband and son. My parents rarely socialized with anyone because my dad was so mean, but they were the one family from church he always wanted to hang out with, and my mom began to notice that her hairdresser was often at the parsonage. She was supposed to be Mom's best friend.

A few weeks after we started at Mr. Chapel's, Mom and Jefferson began looking for more work. We had a roof over our heads, but we still needed a way to make actual money. They took me with them to the local farm labor office, little more than a trailer near the highway. A woman inside sat at a table. She was smoking a cigarette and thumbing through a box of well-worn index cards.

"How can I help you folks?" she asked. "You look new."

"Yes ma'am, we are *brand* new," Jefferson replied. "They said you might be able to help us find work."

"Well, now," the woman replied, pausing to take a drag of her cigarette. "Let me see what I can do."

As she flipped through her cards, she chatted lightly with Jefferson. She had only one leg. She said her name was Marge.

"Can you do farm work?" she asked.

"Girl!" Jefferson exclaimed. "I've done farm work my whole life. I was raised on a farm."

"Well, it's still early for raspberries. You and your wife could do that, even the boy. There's also hay. She snuffed out her smoke and looked across the table.

"Why don't you head over to Cameron Farm? They've got some early strawberries. The work ain't easy, but it pays."

The day we spent in the strawberry fields still stands as one of the hardest of my life. Everyone but us was an immigrant farm worker. Take it from me, there's no harder job than picking strawberries. If you sit down, you can't move along the rows. If you stand, you can't reach the fruit. The only way to pick strawberries with any success is to squat. When pain engulfs your body, you know you're in the right position.

In the fields, small groups spread out and picked as much fruit as they could as fast as they could. Payment depended on how much you harvested. Years after our day among the strawberry rows, Mom still liked to remind me how I whined the entire time. As I recall, so did she. Of the three of us, the only one who was any good at picking strawberries was Jefferson, and he didn't complain once. In fact, I think he might have been whistling or singing.

Mom enrolled me in Sequim Middle School. Less than two months remained before summer. I avoided other kids as much as possible because we feared being discovered. As the weeks passed, I noticed how late the sun stayed out. By June, I could see across the ranch until past ten o'clock.

We continued to make a home for ourselves at Mr. Chapel's place. Jefferson built a coffee table from a sheet of plywood and two tree trunks. Mom finished it with dark stain and hummingbird decals. With the start of summer, we also began exploring the mountains above us. We'd leave straight from the caretaker's residence and hike until the sky turned pink. Our best walks took us to viewpoints overlooking the Strait of Juan de Fuca and Vancouver Island.

We drove down Blue Mountain Road almost every day. At the bottom we stopped at a small grocery store beside the highway. On the way, we often saw a group of kids playing outside an old farmhouse. One day a woman who lived next door to the farmhouse waved us down. Jefferson pulled over, and mom rolled down the window.

"I hear you're staying at the Chapel ranch," the woman said. She introduced herself and her kids, and she invited Mom and Jefferson in for coffee. Our families became quick friends. When they asked us to their church, Jefferson was elated. The first time we went, his voice dominated the sanctuary. We began to attend regularly and made more friends. When people asked where we were from, we told them Missouri. None of us felt good about lying.

One Sunday they asked Jefferson to preach. Jefferson almost always sang a song at the end of his sermon, especially when he was filled with the Holy Spirit. I remember the song he sang that day, one of my favorites. "I . . . Love the Lord, I love the Lord. I . . . Love the Lord, he brought me out and saved me from my sins. I love the Lord." No one in this all-white congregation, located in the farthest northwest corner of the United States you could possibly be in, had ever heard anything like it. Immediately after, you could hear only silence, and then Jefferson received lots of "amens" and everyone seemed happy to have him there.

But a short time later, the full-time pastor explained to us that because Jefferson was Black and not properly ordained in this church denomination, he couldn't preach anymore. The reality was that with our family makeup, we couldn't escape racism anywhere in the United States. While it was more nuanced in Sequim than it was in Kansas, it was still here nonetheless.

Lavender fields in Sequim's Dungeness Valley

Mom called Grandpa weekly. He said Dad hadn't stopped looking for us and that he had been given legal custody of me. It was
strange to think about. In some ways, Dad already seemed like a distant memory. In other ways, he lurked around every corner waiting
to pounce.

Jefferson continued to visit Marge at the farm labor extension office.
When a full-time position opened at Graysmarsh Farm, she told him
about it. Soon afterward, we left Blue Mountain. Mr. Chapel was
sorry to see us go, but he knew we couldn't turn down the opportunity. The new job came with a house *and* a paycheck. We thanked
Mr. Chapel for everything he'd done. I doubt he ever realized how
crucial he was to our family's survival.

Graysmarsh Farm was a registered Guernsey dairy and one of
the largest berry-picking operations in the country. It was also home
to abundant wildlife. Jefferson milked cows and did odd jobs around
the farm. Along with steady pay and half a duplex on the main Graysmarsh property, we also received all the free milk we could drink.

Around this time, I started seventh grade. I also began to think
less about Kansas. I still wasn't supposed to tell anyone where we'd
come from, but it didn't seem to matter. We'd made it. Dad had no
idea where we were.

Jefferson worked long hours on the farm, I went to school, and
Mom managed the house. She worked hard to make the duplex feel
like home. She painted and put up bright wallpaper, and she uphol-
stered an old couch in red velvet. We didn't have much money, but we
didn't need a lot either. We were close to the beach, and the three of
us often went there on weekends to walk Trixie and drag driftwood
from the surf. We had a roof over our heads. More important, we
were free from violence. I was even making friends at school.

In Sequim, our family was different from everyone else and that made us special. People still stared, but we couldn't fault them for it. Many had never seen a Black man before, let alone a mixed-race couple. People were understandably curious. Most were also kind. In November of 1970, as we sat down to our first Thanksgiving in Sequim, we had plenty of reasons to express gratitude. Gone were fear and abuse. We had escaped Dad and Kansas and racial violence—and everything else that once had held us back. Together, we had begun a new life. In the course of seven months, our futures had changed. As Jefferson said grace before dinner, I finally felt safe.

CHAPTER FOUR

Don't Forget Me

November 30, 1970, dawned cold. It was the Monday after Thanksgiving. At school most of the kids stayed inside. Back in Kansas, we would have considered the same day warm for late November. In Edwardsville Mom and I had often played outside after a winter storm, when thick blankets of snow smothered the landscape. One time, Dad joined us and we tossed snowballs playfully and fell to the ground to make snow angels with our bundled bodies. I was excited when Dad came out to play. During every moment of fun, I hoped it was the beginning of more moments; I wished it would last.

It seems ironic that I would think about Kansas that cold Monday after Thanksgiving. I remember standing at my locker between classes, and I can still feel the tap on my shoulder as I turned to see the principal and a police officer behind me. I froze. I think some small part of me knew this moment would come. As much as I wanted to believe Dad had stopped looking for me, I knew it wasn't true. As long as Mom and I were free and living with Jefferson, he wouldn't rest. For him, giving up would mean losing. More than that, it would mean perceived social shame wherever he went. He needed control. It was important that he not feel embarrassed at all costs, and we were embarrassments.

When I first reentered the school system, Mom had walked into the administrative office and enrolled me as Scott Jackson, my new identity. But later in the day after she had left, the office summoned me to obtain more details for ordering my records from my prior school. When they asked me what name my records would be under, I gave them my real name. So either my former school called the police or the police were tracking the school right from the beginning.

That Monday after Thanksgiving, walking from my locker toward the principal's office, I felt as if Dad were dragging me by the ear. Every kid in the hall stared. A few minutes later, looking out the back of a patrol car, I saw my classmates press their faces against classroom windows and watch me disappear. An hour later, I entered a juvenile detention center on the far outskirts of Port Angeles. During the drive, two plain-clothed officials bracketed me in the backseat. They told me Mom was being notified of my whereabouts and that she was facing contempt of court charges and likely would face kidnapping charges. They also said I'd be sent back to Kansas.

Built of cement and ash-colored stucco, the detention center looked like a fortress. In the lobby, a guard emptied my pockets and led me further into the building to a small room with a single bed. It was late afternoon by the time Mom and Jefferson arrived. Mom's eyes were red, and Jefferson looked disheartened.

"I'm so sorry," Mom said through tears. "I don't know what we could have done . . ."

Her voice trailed off. Jefferson held her hand as she struggled to find her words. She was still crying when I asked how they found out I'd been taken. A police officer had knocked on the door of the duplex and told her, and she had run barefoot to find Jefferson. They drove as fast as they could to meet me but were forced to wait. That's when they found a lawyer.

They didn't get a chance to tell me much more. The guard only allowed us a few minutes before interrupting. As Mom and Jefferson left, I walked back to my new room. That night I ate dinner in the cafeteria with a boy from a nearby Indian reservation. I remember thinking he was bigger than me. He had dark skin and a long black braid that hung down his back. He grew up on the coast, but his parents had died. His foster parents hit him, so he ran away. When he got caught stealing he ended up in the detention center.

Two days after I was taken from school, Mom and Jefferson entered a courtroom in Port Angeles. Across the aisle, Dad sat in silence. In the hall a police officer stood next to me as I strained to hear the judge. Attorney Brooke Taylor argued our case. Mom and Jefferson had found him in a small office above a bank in downtown Port Angeles, and he quickly accepted them as clients. Taylor was twenty-seven years old and less than two years out of law school. He had recently been elected county prosecuting attorney but had yet to take office. Our case struck a chord with the young lawyer.

Taylor had had only a few hours to prepare since meeting Mom and Jefferson. From outside the courtroom, I could hear him argue that the Kansas order giving Dad custody was racist and that the court had no legal reason to take me from Mom. I also heard him tell the judge about Dad's abuse.

That night in the detention center, I stared at the ceiling of my room and let the tears stream down my face. The next morning, Taylor filed a motion to stay the proceedings pending an appeal. He argued that by upholding the Kansas order, the court would strip Mom of all parental rights. The judge didn't budge. As his gavel crashed, Dad finally won.

Dad left the courtroom first.

"Scottie," he said, stopping in the hall. "I know this must be hard for you. . . ."

I began to feel ill. His mouth was still moving, but I couldn't hear him. My head began to spin, my stomach burned, and I wanted to scream. My throat was too dry to speak. I thought I might collapse, and I stared at the floor to steady myself. When I looked up again, I saw his back as the outside door closed behind him.

Mom and Jefferson appeared next. Tears poured from Mom's eyes. She could barely speak. "I'm so sorry. We tried."

Jefferson put his hand on my shoulder.

"It's not over, Boy. We'll keep fighting." His grip felt strong. I believed him.

Mom composed herself. Then they told me an appeal was still possible. Brooke Taylor said he would continue working on our case. A higher court might reconsider the Kansas ruling, something this judge refused to do. For now, I had to return to Kansas.

On Sunday morning, Mom and Jefferson came for their final visit at the detention center.

"We'll keep fighting," mom said. "And I'll write to you every day."

I believed her. As we spoke, a guard stood outside the visitors' room. Mom grabbed my hand and squeezed hard. "People are praying for you," she said.

Then she began to whisper. "We have something for you. Something you need to keep close." She reached into her purse and handed me a Bible. She flipped it open, and I saw the names and phone numbers of old friends and contacts from Kansas and across the country written in light pencil. She turned to Psalm 23. Grandma and Grandpa Hughes' phone number appeared in the margin.

"Just in case," Mom said.

I didn't understand what she meant. Before I could ask, she handed me a dark green knit hat. "A woman in the church made this special hat for you," she said.

It looked warm. But there was something else. Leaning over, Mom gently pulled back some of the stitching. Between layers of yarn I saw money sewn inside. When she let go, the double stitching and green yarn made it invisible again.

Suddenly I was crying.

"What do you want me to do?" I asked.

"You need to do what's right," Mom said softly. "No matter what, we'll be here."

Then our time was up. The guard entered to take me back to my room. I hugged Mom and Jefferson with all the strength I had. I didn't want to let go. I never wanted to let go.

"We love you," Jefferson said through tears.

"I love you, too," I said. "Don't forget me."

On Monday morning a woman brought a folded pile of clothes to my room at the detention center. I dressed slowly. When I arrived in the lobby, Dad stood up.

"Hi, Scottie." That was all he could say before I exploded.

"Go to hell, you bastard. You don't want me."

I wanted to punch him in the face. I wanted to take every bit of anger I had and throw it at him. What could he do? We were still inside the detention center. He wouldn't dare hit me in front of witnesses. But who was I kidding? He weighed a hundred pounds more than me— by this time, my dad had become obese. Even if he didn't hit me here, he'd certainly make me pay later. *Not now,* I told myself. *Not like this.*

The drive to Kansas passed slowly. For much of the trip I refused to speak. Every time we stopped, I looked for ways to run away. When we pulled off the interstate for food and gas, Dad followed me to the bathroom. Every hour in the car seemed like another eternity away from Sequim. Four days after leaving Port Angeles, Dad pulled up the gravel drive in front of Tall Oaks. As he did, a crash of memories collapsed around me. Everything looked exactly the same.

I returned to school in Linwood. I'd been gone less than a year. Rather than nostalgia, I felt apathy. Dad picked me up each after-noon. I wasn't allowed to ride the bus. If Dad couldn't make it on time, he sent Slim, the camp handyman. I couldn't leave the house alone. The one thing I could do was play basketball in the yard.

A few weeks after we got back, Dad said, "I think you need to see a counselor. You've been through a lot."

"I don't need a counselor," I argued. "I just need my mother."

"Well, we're going to see this counselor; the courts are requiring it, and it will be good for you."

"Don't make me see a counselor—you'll regret it," I threatened.

We took the elevator up a few floors and walked into the waiting room. Chairs with green cushions were lined up against the wall, in front of which stood a table with a selection of magazines. A woman came out to greet us and asked me to come in while Dad remained in the waiting room. She had brunette hair, glasses, a medium build, and a round face. She looked safe enough initially, but when she began to speak, I knew I couldn't trust her.

She said, "So I understand you may be having a hard time now that you're back with your real dad. That's natural, especially with the additional complications of being with your mom and a Black man. I'm here to help you talk about that." She went on about how she felt bad for me that I had to spend time with Mom and Jefferson and felt it was important to make adjustments, talk about it, and reenter the white world. "It must have been tough living with a Black man," she sympathized.

Jefferson and Sydney Lou

"Listen, you bitch, there was nothing hard about living with Jefferson and my mom," I spewed. "That man out there beat my mom. You can send me back to the fucking judge and I'm going to tell him what you said and how prejudiced you are and that my dad is a wife beater, and I don't need any goddamned counseling from you."

Then I picked up a side table and threw it across the room. She walked out to the waiting room and finally came back, and then we left.

Dad said, "You'll never have to see another counselor again." We never went back.

I saw Grandma and Grandpa a few weeks after my return to Kansas. They came to Tall Oaks with Ricky and Patty early one afternoon just before Christmas. Grandma had baked a cake, and they brought me some pictures of Mom and Jefferson taken in Sequim after I left. They brought me a small artificial Christmas tree with handmade baked ornaments of all of them, reminding me of our life in Sequim. Dad inspected everything before I could have it. That evening, as I walked the four of them to their car, Grandpa asked if I had received any of Mom's letters. I hadn't.

"Listen," I said, "you have to get me out of here."

"We will, Scottie, but we don't know much more about the courts and the appeal your mom is trying to make, but she's trying. So don't lose hope."

"Well, I won't, but isn't there anything else we can do? Because he has a gun underneath his bed and I don't want to be here."

"What kind of gun?" Grandpa Whitey asked.

"A handgun," I replied.

"Has he brought it out to you? Has he hit you?"

"No, not really, but I don't feel comfortable here."

Shortly after they left, the police showed up at the office door and Dad answered. They told him they'd received a complaint that he had a gun and his son was scared for his life, and they came in and questioned us. My father was livid.

As winter settled over Kansas and Tall Oaks, I felt the cold sting of distance between Mom, Jefferson, and me. With it came the realization that I wasn't thinking about them as much. Instead, I was starting to adjust to life with Dad. I started to doubt how much they could do. Nearly two months had passed and I still hadn't received a single letter. I didn't think they had given up—I knew something was wrong because my grandfather had told me my mom had been writing to me—but with each week, the memories started to fade. And I was guarded all the time. My dad rarely left me alone. I knew it was pretty hopeless and didn't think Mom and Jefferson could get a court appeal. Who was going to listen to a white woman and a Black man? My memories would fade, and my reality became the reality of living there. I was afraid I was going to forget my mom.

Kansas was home now, after all.

CHAPTER FIVE

I Love You

My decision to run away began with a trip to the post office. That afternoon, Dad picked me up from school, parked outside the tiny post office in Linwood, and told me to wait in the car. I could see the service counter through the large outside windows. Because it was snowing, and because I was cold, and maybe because I just wanted to get Dad mad, I waited only a few minutes before going in. By the time Dad noticed, it was too late. He tried to shuffle the envelope to the bottom of his stack, but I'd already seen Mom's handwriting.

"Hey, that's mine," I yelled. "Give me that."

The post office clerk turned toward me and back to Dad. I knew instantly I had committed a mortal sin. I'd embarrassed my father in public. Dad turned his entire body toward me. His face warped, his teeth clenched, and I could see him start to shake.

"Get in the car," he ordered. His voice sounded intense, measured, staccato.

He stepped toward me. I backed away. "Move!" he yelled.

On the ride home, Dad remained silent. I knew not to speak when he got this way. I wouldn't wait long. He had something I wanted, and I'd do anything to get it. Inside the house, I followed him to the kitchen.

In a start, he turned and yelled, "Go to your room. Now!"

He towered over me. He looked exactly like he had so many times before when I'd watched him hit Mom or bang on the bathroom door as she cried inside. I knew he'd hit me if I didn't move. I slumped away and started toward the hall. Just once, I looked back. Dad had set the mail on the counter and started to take off his coat. I lunged for the envelope. When I felt it between my fingers I started to run. Dad charged after me. I darted down the hall and turned into my room. But I was too slow. Dad's weight crashed on top of me. His fury landed with a heavy thud, and my arm slammed against the bedpost. My body shuddered as he pinned me to the floor. His fist smashed against my ribs. Pain tore through me. Dad's immense weight felt as though it might kill me. Just then, Dad grabbed the letter from my hand, got up, and slammed the door.

My head spun like the snow swirling outside. Memories flashed to mind: *Mom and Jefferson walking in the hills above Sequim and sitting in a field at dusk . . . Dad choking Mom and throwing her against a wall . . . The bright light of a single train rushing toward me down the tracks near the old parsonage in Edwardsville.*

I don't recall everything I thought about in those few moments. More than anything, I was scared. Scared of Dad. Scared I'd never see Mom again. Scared of what would happen next.

I was still sitting on the floor when Dad returned to my room. His body filled the doorway.

"Here's your stupid letter." He threw it on my bed and walked away.

On the outside of the envelope, Mom's handwriting looked just as I remembered. I began to imagine all the things she must have written. She would tell me about her and Jefferson, about Sequim, and about our friends from church. I picked up the envelope and reached inside. A single sheet of paper came out. Unfolding it, I saw only three words: *I love you.*

I felt stunned. That was *it?* Didn't she have anything else to say? Did she even care about me anymore? I'd hoped Mom's letter would bring some kind of relief. Instead it only confused me. As I lay in my room, aching, I realized something. In that moment, silent and in pain, staring at the ceiling, I grasped the reality before me. I'd had my suspicions. I suppose that's why I went into the post office to begin with. But now I knew for sure. Ever since I had been back, Dad had been keeping my mail from me. Mom wrote only three words because she knew Dad wouldn't let me read anything else.

I began to move almost as soon as I had the thought. Since my return to Kansas, I'd been careful to keep the Bible and knit cap Mom had given me away from Dad. Now I reached under my bed and pulled the Bible from its hiding spot. Inside my closet, I grabbed a duffel bag and put my basketball inside. It was the same one I ran away with the first time. Mom and Jefferson had left it for me after their final visit to the detention center in Port Angeles. I moved quickly around my room to get some underwear, a sweatshirt, a couple of comic books, and the knit cap stored carefully on the top shelf of my closet. I zipped up the duffel, and then walked to my window and dropped the bag into the snow.

I could jump out the window easily and be okay. But if I did and Dad came looking for me, I wouldn't get far. I closed the window, pulled on my heaviest coat, stuffed the cap into one of my pockets. I headed down the hall where I found Dad in his office.

"Sorry about the letter," I said. "I shouldn't have done that. Anyway, I guess she didn't have much to say."

Dad looked up at me. "I guess not."

"Can I go for a walk? I want to see the snow. I won't go far."

Maybe he felt bad about hitting me, or maybe he just realized he couldn't keep me in my room forever. "Stay close," he said. "It's getting dark."

Stepping outside, I pulled on the knit cap. Cold air bit at my face as I circled back to my bedroom window to retrieve the duffel. I slung it over my shoulder and hurried across the yard. I skirted some nearby trees and made a beeline for the camp mess hall. Fresh snow covered the ground. I left a trail of tennis shoe tracks behind me.

The door to the commons swung open easily. It was empty inside. I walked straight to the payphone. The number was written inside my Bible, but I didn't need to look.

"Scottie, is that you?" Grandpa's voice came from the other end of the line.

"Yes. I'm running away. I want to go home. I want to go back to Sequim." My voice sounded anxious. "It's snowing. I don't know what to do."

"Hold on. Don't go anywhere. I'll be right back." Grandpa set down the phone. Across the mess hall, I heard pots clang. Someone was in the kitchen. Before I could react, Grandpa came back on the line.

"Listen carefully, Scottie. Do you remember the horse ranch in De Soto? We bought Midnight there. It's about five miles from you. Can you get there?"

I remembered the ranch and the day Mom and Grandpa took me there. I didn't know where it was, but I knew how to get to De Soto. It wouldn't be easy in the snow, but I didn't have a choice.

"I can get there," I said. "I'll find the ranch."

"When you do, knock on the door. Tell them Whitey sent you. Say your ride is late because of the snow. A car will come pick you up. You'll hear three honks. That will be your signal to leave."

More sounds from the kitchen.

"Grandpa, I have to go." I was whispering now.

"We love you, Scottie. Be safe. We'll see you soon."

I hung up the phone quietly and turned for the door. I moved quickly back outside. Looking down, I realized my feet were already wet from snow seeping through my tennis shoes.

The main camp road ran through the property about a hundred feet west of the dining hall. I ran straight toward it and kept on running. Beyond the road, the oak forest provided cover. Even without leaves, the trees created a nice hiding place. I didn't know how long Dad would let me stay outside before he came looking. Not long, I thought. I moved beyond the edge of the woods to deeper cover.

Looking up, I saw a tangled braid of Black branches against a dark gray sky. Soft light was reflected from the falling snow.

Suddenly, I heard a rustling. When I turned, two dark eyes stared straight through me. A second later the deer darted through the trees. I followed its lead. My heart raced. I told myself to keep going until I reached the swimming pool, about a hundred yards up the road.

A chain-link fence surrounded the pool. Beyond it, a hill sloped downward away from the road. I stopped to listen. Quiet. I began to run again, this time toward the open-air chapel farther down the road. *One step at a time. Point to point. Keep moving.*

At the chapel, I again stopped to listen. Nothing. I looked up at the swooping limestone wall and the tall cross that hung from one side. I used to sit in the chapel alone and pray. I'd pray that Dad would stop hitting Mom and that everything would get better. Those prayers never came true. At times I questioned why God had put me in this situation, but I never gave up on my faith. Before I left, I said another quick prayer, the kind you think more than say. *Amen.*

Again I began running.

Back in the woods, I moved quickly toward the bluff near the end of the camp road. I ran hard. I began to breathe heavily. I heard something behind me. I stopped and turned my head. A truck was driving up the road. I could hear it struggling in the snow. I knew it could only be Dad or Slim. I turned back for the bluff and moved deeper into the trees.

I reached the top of the hill well ahead of the truck. Looking down the bluff, I knew this was my last chance to turn around, to create some kind of story about why I had come this far. If I went any farther and got caught, there would be no hiding my motive. I feared what Dad might do when he found me. It didn't matter. I already felt free. Even if the feeling didn't last, I wasn't going to give it up willingly. There was a stillness that settled upon me.

The quiet that surrounded me was more than the ensuing darkness, more than the deafening silence of snow falling, and even more than the hissing sound of the wind. I reached up with my arm and felt the knit hat with the twenty dollar bills sewn inside and adjusted it down over my ears to prevent frostbite from the cold.

I stared across the open distance in front of me. A wide snow-covered field ran along the bottom of the bluff. Beyond was the road to De Soto. From where the field met the road I figured it was about two miles to the Wyandotte Street Bridge. The bridge crossed the Kansas River into De Soto.

The rumble of the truck snapped me to attention. I looked back just once before darting over the edge of the bluff. As the slope steepened, I began to slide. The snow caused me to move uncontrollably. My tennis shoes provided little traction. Thick bushes tore at my coat.

It took less than a minute to reach the field. Somehow I made it without falling. It was almost completely dark now. I looked back up the bluff. The sound of the truck had stopped. Between the road and me stood only untracked snow. I took off as fast as I could through the shallow snow. Midway across the field I collapsed. A sharp pain shot through my left leg. I rolled on the ground wincing. I tore off my shoe. Blood seeped from my heel. My toes froze. A large thorn stuck through my sock. It somehow had found its way down the side of my shoe before lodging in the bottom of my foot. I squinted back toward the bluff. Darkness was my ally. Anyone standing atop the slope would struggle to see me. Anyone driving by on the road would likely miss me in the snow and dusky light.

My foot throbbed. *No time.* I pulled out the thorn, retied my shoe, and again started to move. Cold air stung my lungs. I reached up and pulled my hat down over my ears.

I arrived at the road and crossed straight to the other side. A thin strip of land separated the street from the railroad berm and tracks. Up and over, I disappeared on the other side of the embankment. A narrow band of trees ran along the riverbank. Through it I heard the soft lapping of water against the shore. I was exactly where I wanted to be. The rail berm hid me from the road, and I could follow the tracks toward De Soto. This was my territory, the exact kind of spot where I spent endless hours when back in Edwardsville; I roamed the north shore of the same river, the same tracks.

A faint glow of light hung low in the distant vespertine sky. Catching my breath, I thought about Mom and Jefferson. *What would they think if they knew where I was? Has Grandpa called them? Are they wondering about me right now?* The cold air snapped me back to the present moment.

There was only one way to get to De Soto: the Wyandotte Street Bridge. Almost instinctively, I reached up and touched my hat. Pinching it, I felt the money sewn inside. The snowfall had nearly stopped, and a cold wind blew undiluted down the tracks. I pulled the hat tighter over my ears. My left foot still stung. I didn't know how long it would take for Grandpa's connection, whoever it was, to drive to the horse ranch, but I knew I needed to get there first.

I started jogging east along the edge of the tracks. The snow cover was lighter here than in the field. After a few minutes, the tracks crossed a small stream that ran toward the river. From here, it was about a mile and a half to Wyandotte Street. I kept moving along the bottom of the berm, watching for spikes and other debris in the near darkness. The sound of an engine startled me. It came from the road. I stopped. Whoever it was, they were driving slowly. I lowered my body and climbed the rail berm. In the distance, I saw flashing red and blue police lights. I kept my head to the tracks and watched as the car moved closer.

What are they doing? Are they looking for me? The answers seemed obvious.

I dropped back down to the berm. If someone climbed up the other side, they'd spot me easily. I considered giving up. If I turned myself in, maybe Dad wouldn't be upset. I was colder and colder. I had left around four o'clock and it was now dark. I had been walking for hours. I questioned my decision to run away. The thought of trying to find a horse ranch in a town I barely knew began to scare me. *Is it crazy to keep going? Climb over the tracks. You'll be safe. You'll be warm.*

I shook my head in disbelief. What was wrong with me? Dad had just tackled and punched me. Things weren't going to get any better, especially now. I looked toward the faint glow of De Soto. Across the tracks, the flashing lights passed parallel to my position and continued toward Wyandotte Street. As the lights dimmed, I started moving again. The junction of the tracks and Wyandotte Street grew closer with each step. There was only one way to cross the river. *It's a trap.*

It didn't matter. I was out of options. If I couldn't cross the bridge, I couldn't run away. I reached Wyandotte Street about fifteen minutes later. *It's over.*

I looked up at the night sky. Not a single star broke the clouds. I shook my head. *Kansas is home now.*

I climbed the berm slowly to meet my fate. Standing at the junction of the tracks and Wyandotte Street, I looked around. The police lights were gone. Darkness and empty fields surrounded me. To the south, the glow of De Soto appeared brighter across the river.

I began to walk toward the light, keeping a few yards off the street and hugging sparse hedgerows. As I did, I found myself humming a song Jefferson had taught me.

> *We've come this far by faith,*
> *leaning on the Lord;*
> *trusting in His holy word.*
> *He's never failed us yet.*
> *Oh! We can't turn back,*
> *We've come this far by faith.*

I knew I was doing the right thing. Even if I got caught, I had to try to get back to Mom and Jefferson. They'd given up almost everything they had to escape with me the first time. I owed it to them to get back.

Suddenly, headlights appeared behind me. Turning around, I could tell immediately it was a truck. *I'm doomed!*

Part of me wanted to run, but there was no place to go. The only thing on either side of the road was an open field covered in snow. As the truck came closer, I froze. A second later, I realized it wasn't the camp truck. Mixed thoughts raced through my mind. *Lay on the ground. Hide. No. Wait.*

Before I knew it, I was standing in the road waving my arms. The truck stopped. I walked to the passenger-side door. An old man dressed in blue overalls leaned across the bench seat and rolled down the window. I had no idea what to say. I was alone at night in the middle of a storm. He must have thought I was crazy. Maybe I was. Whose idea was it to run away in a storm?

"Can I get a lift to the city limits? I didn't realize how cold it was when I started." My words came without thought. The man looked like he was trying to decide if I was real or some sort of icy hallucination.

"The city limits?" he asked.

"Yeah. I'm meeting a friend."

"Alright. Jump in."

He put the truck in gear and started toward the bridge. The road was slick, and his wheels spun before finding traction. We didn't talk much. I was glad he didn't ask any more questions. It took only a few minutes to cross the bridge and enter De Soto.

"Here you are," he said, pulling over. "You sure I can't take you any farther?"

"No, this is perfect." I opened the door and jumped out. "Thanks."

As he pulled away, I began to walk away from the river. A couple of blocks later, I reached the main road through town. Warm yellow light blazed through the windows of a nearby café. Inside the small restaurant heat surrounded me. A few patrons looked up briefly before returning to their dinner. I quickly saw what I needed. The payphone didn't interest me, but the phonebook did. I flipped through the yellow pages and found the ranch. Spotting the waitress nearby, I asked if she knew how to get there.

"It's not far," she smiled, offering directions. "Keep your eye out. It might be hard to see in the storm."

Outside, the snow was falling more heavily. I pulled my collar up against the cold. It took almost an hour to reach the ranch on the outskirts of town. During that time, not a single car passed on the road. If anyone were to travel this forsaken, snow-covered country road, I would see them but they would not see me.

The ranch looked just as I remembered. A large single-story home, a huge barn, fenced horse rings, and big empty fields now covered in white. I made my way up the driveway to the steps and covered front porch and rang the bell. I had walked twelve miles to get here.

A man about Grandpa's age opened the door and looked down at me. I recognized his face from the day we bought Midnight. I could tell from his expression he was surprised to see me. I began to rush through my cover story.

The man didn't let me talk long. Maybe he realized how cold I was outside. Standing on his front porch, I began to feel the chill sink in. The walk must have helped keep me warm, because I was suddenly shivering. I had walked for four or five hours.

Inside, the man asked me to take off my coat and sit down. Then he disappeared to tell his wife they had company. As he did, I took a deep breath. I'd done it. I'd made it from Tall Oaks to the horse ranch without getting caught. It seemed like forever since I'd hung up the phone in the camp mess hall. Now I had a new worry: *Where's my ride?*

When the ranch owner returned, I was standing by a large window looking over the driveway and front yard. His wife stood next to him. She said hello and asked if I wanted cookies and hot chocolate. A few minutes later she found me on the couch, watching TV with her husband. As the minutes ticked by, I grew increasingly anxious. *What if no one comes? How long until these people start to ask questions? Do they know Dad?*

Suddenly, I heard a honk. I looked out the front window and saw headlights in the driveway.

"That's my ride," I said. "Thank you so much."

Stepping off the front porch, I wondered who was in the car. The back door cracked open as I approached. I strained to look inside. Just before I got in I heard the ranch owner's voice behind me: "Tell your Grandpa we said hello."

From inside the car, a deep voice said, "Hurry. Get in."

The driver wasn't alone. Someone else sat in the passenger seat. Glancing over his shoulder, I could see he was holding a shotgun across his lap.

Who are these people? Why should I trust them?

I had little time to think about the answers.

"Lay down. Don't talk. We don't want anyone to know you're back there."

I did what the driver said. As we drove away, I started to pray.

After a few minutes, the driver spoke again.

"Don't worry, Scottie. We're going to get you to your Grandpa."

At least he knows my name.

"If anyone stops us, you're a hitchhiker. We picked you up in the snow. Got it?"

Lying on my back across the seat, I could see the snow falling again. The car moved slowly. I could hear the wiper blades. We were headed toward the Missouri state line. *We're going in the right direction.*

I stayed low and listened as the two men up front started to relax. They spoke in low voices; their tension seemed to be easing.

During the ride, I moved through stages of feeling worried and feeling liberated. Listening to the men talk to each other seemed to help. They were on a mission. On the other hand, thinking about the gun freaked me out. My escape had quickly become more dangerous than I imagined. *What if we're pulled over? Will they shoot a police officer?*

"I'm Jerry, by the way." It was the driver. Looking up, I saw the side of his face in the faint light. "You're doing great back there. Your Grandpa and I go way back. Stay low. The city's coming up."

Nearly an hour elapsed between De Soto and the state line. In good weather the drive would have taken half as long. I never learned the other man's name. As we crossed the border, Jerry said I could sit up as long as I crouched low enough so no one could see me. I began to recognize some of the roads. Crossing the Missouri River, I thought about the last time I visited Grandma and Grandpa's house. It was the night Mom and Jefferson planned our escape—my first escape. The river seemed larger than I recalled. I started to think about some of the times Mom and I drove to Claycomo to get away from Dad. I remembered Mom's bruises, her tears, and how afraid she used to get. Years later I'd learn more about the abuse, about how Mom's friends took her in during those nights she ran from our house, about the bite marks and bruises they saw during those frightening times when they found their friend Sydney at their front door crying and wearing only a nightgown.

"Scottie!" Jerry's voice snapped me back to the moment. "We're here. North Kansas City. I'm going to drop you off at city hall. Don't worry. Your Grandpa's waiting inside."

I was shocked. *City hall? That makes no sense. What are we doing here?*

"What?" I asked.

Jerry hesitated. "Trust me."

"But it's the middle of the night."

"I know. Just trust me."

"Will I see you again?"

"I hope so."

I didn't know much about North Kansas City. Mom went to high school nearby. Grandpa surely knew people here. Beyond that, I only knew it was across the river from Kansas City.

Jerry stopped the car. I grabbed my bag and got out reluctantly.

City hall was a short nondescript building with a large parking lot. Following Jerry's instructions, I walked toward the front door. I didn't feel good about this plan at all. The snow had stopped, and an eerie quiet floated through the air. As I approached the building, Grandpa opened the front door and walked outside. He wore a dark suit and looked serious. Behind him I saw Grandma and Ricky. I could hardly believe it. They rushed past Grandpa. Somewhere between the parking lot and the front doors we collided in a group hug.

Grandpa brought us to attention.

"Listen. We're going inside to talk to a friend. He's a lawyer. Don't worry."

Grandpa's command of the situation relieved me. Standing in front of city hall seemed like the worst possible place to be. But Grandpa Whitey knew what he was doing. Anyway, it seemed that way. At that moment, that was good enough.

We moved quickly inside, down the halls. Turning into one of the offices, I saw a man sitting alone behind a huge desk. Like Grandpa, he wore a dark suit. He began to speak quickly. At first, he recapped what I already knew: Dad had full custody of me; Mom and Jefferson were lucky to avoid kidnapping charges; the Kansas court didn't want anything else to do with our case.

What he said next hit me like an important newsflash: "Your mom won an appeal in Washington. I have no idea how she pulled it off. She must have one hell of an attorney. There's just one problem. The decision has no effect here. Unless you get back to Washington, your dad still has legal custody."

A train could have driven straight through that office and I would have been less shocked. *Mom won! She and Jefferson did exactly what they said they would. They kept fighting for me.*

The attorney turned to Grandpa and offered a smile. "Whitey, you're playing with fire here. There's a warrant pending to search your house. The fact is no court in Kansas or Missouri will side with an unknown judge out West. Not on this."

I felt a new wave of anxiety. If I got caught now, I would find myself right back at Tall Oaks. Only now it would be worse. Dad would lock me down completely. The thought was unbearable.

Grandpa thanked his friend, and we left as quickly as we had arrived. Back outside, Grandpa steered his Cadillac away from city hall. I kept my head low in the backseat. As we drove toward Clay-como, Grandpa hatched a plan.

"You can't come home with us tonight, Scottie," he said. "We're going to drop you at Bill's place. You can stay with him and Dixie. You'll be safe there. Tomorrow you're going back to Sequim."

I'd met Bill Edwards many times around Grandpa's store, but had never been to his house. I didn't know Dixie, his wife, at all. It didn't matter. Driving through the outskirts of Kansas City with Grandma and Grandpa, I started to get the feeling everything would work out.

The police car changed those feelings instantly. Grandpa had taken the main road through Claycomo and driven right past the farm. Across the property, a police cruiser was parked in the drive-way. Grandma spotted it first.

"Scottie! Get on the floor!"

Grandpa's decision to drive that close to the house seemed crazy, which Grandma made sure to tell him. I stayed glued to the backseat for the rest of the ride. Grandpa looked repeatedly in his mirrors to see if we were being followed. When the car stopped, I sat up and looked out the window.

Bill Edwards and my mom had gone to school together. In high school, Bill worked at Grandpa's store. Grandpa took him in as a sort of protégé. Bill later opened his own business and bought property around Claycomo, growing into one of the area's wealthier residents.

"It all started at Hughes Furniture," Grandpa had said more than once.

He turned to look at me in the backseat. "We love you, Scottie. You did great tonight. Now go on. They know you're coming."

No long goodbye. Just a smile and a wave. Too much still on the line. Grandma was still upset about Whitey's risk driving by the farm.

Bill and Dixie answered the front door together. I saw my grandparents and Ricky drive away as it closed. I didn't know when I would see them again. But I didn't have time to think about it. Bill showed me around the house, and Dixie asked if I wanted any hot chocolate. If nothing else, running away had paid dividends in hot chocolate.

"We're glad you're here," Bill said. "You did the right thing. Your mom is going to be thrilled to see you."

Grandpa trusted Bill more than anyone. He was the only person outside our family who knew where Grandpa stashed his cash around the store and farm. Now he was being trusted with something even more important.

"How do you feel about sleeping in the attic?" Bill asked. "There's a bed up there, and it's a good place to hide. Just in case."

The truth was that nowhere would be completely safe until I got back to Sequim. Even then, there was no telling which court decision would ultimately win out. Right now, though, nothing sounded as good as a bed. I climbed into the attic and fell asleep. Not even Dixie's hot chocolate could wake me.

The sun hadn't yet come up when I awoke. I heard Bill's voice downstairs.

"Time to move, Scottie. Jerry is coming to get you. Dixie is making breakfast."

A few minutes later, still exhausted, I was dressed and watching television. The morning news jolted me. They were talking about me. They gave my name—my real name—my age, and said I was missing. My face flashed across the TV screen.

"Bill! Dixie! I'm on the news. They think I've been kidnapped."

"We have to get you out of here," Bill said, sounding worried. "The sooner you're back with your mom the better."

I scarfed down Dixie's breakfast as fast as I could. Before I finished, I heard Jerry pull up outside.

"Time to go," Bill said. "Jerry will explain everything."

Outside, Jerry motioned to the backseat. This time he was alone. From what I could see, the shotgun was also missing.

"Morning, Scottie." Jerry sounded positively chipper. "Just you and me, kiddo. But I need you to stay down back there."

"Sounds good," I said. "Did you see me on the news?"

"Don't you worry about that. We're getting you out of here."

As we pulled away, Jerry explained the plan.

The drive to Omaha, Nebraska, took four hours. We stopped once to use the restroom. Back in the car, Jerry handed me a white envelope.

"At the airport, I'll go in and pick up your ticket. If anything happens after I leave, do your best to get outside and find me. If you have any problems, use that money. Otherwise give it to your mom."

I opened the envelope. Inside, I saw hundreds of dollars in cash.

"Everything will be okay," Jerry said.

At the airport I waited in a parking lot while Jerry picked up the ticket.

When he returned, he smiled. "You're almost there, Scottie. It's been fun. All you have to do is board the plane. Your mom will be waiting in Seattle."

I couldn't believe it. Less than twenty-four hours had passed since I'd run away from Tall Oaks. Somehow, despite everything, I'd made it this far. I thanked Jerry for all his help and got out of the car.

A few minutes later, walking through the airport, I looked for the quietest spot I could find. When I heard my flight number, I took a quick look around and started for the gate.

Taking off, I noticed how clear the sky was and how beautiful the ground appeared beneath the plane. The storm of yesterday had cleared and in its wake lay below a snowy world of white. It looked just like our front yard outside the parsonage so many years earlier when Mom and Dad and I would go outside and make snow angels and laugh and roll on the ground. How distant the memory seemed. How foreign and irreconcilable with the violence and abuse. Moving west through the blank sky, I put the thought behind me.

A few hours later, peering out the same small window, I saw the Seattle skyline. Inside the airport Mom and Jefferson stood at the gate. They grabbed me, and we hugged for a long time. No one wanted to let go. Mom laughed when she reached for my bag and felt the basketball inside. My good luck charm had worked again.

On the drive home, they told me about the court hearings and how they had won their appeal. They said the fight wasn't over. The appeals court had sent the case back to the county judge for reconsideration—the same judge who sent me back to Kansas.

"This time," Mom said, "he'll have to listen to us."

Her words made me think of something else, something that had happened a few days earlier.

"Thanks for the letter," I said. "I love you, too."

CHAPTER SIX

Sequim—Land of Sunshine

T he Indian meaning for Sequim is something like quiet waters, land of goodness. For me, it will always mean land of sunshine. It was a place where I could be a kid again and learn how to grow up—it was safe. The rich, fertile Dungeness river valley boasts the rugged, snowcapped Olympic Mountains on one side and the deep blue Strait of Juan de Fuca on the other, punctuated with the free-flowing Dungeness River, brimming with silvery flashes of wild salmon and Steelhead trout. Because Sequim sits in the rain shadow of the Olympic Mountains, the Sequim valley only receives an average of sixteen inches of measurable rainfall per year. The well-known farming land is only productive because of an irrigation system connecting the river to the rest of the Dungeness Valley.

I woke suddenly to the sound of voices that first morning back in Sequim. It was early in February 1971. The previous night, Mom and Jefferson had picked me up at the Seattle airport, and we'd driven the two hours back to Sequim, arriving around midnight. They didn't ask about how I ran away. I suppose it didn't matter at the time. What had been the most intense twenty-four hours of my life would, however, remain a lifetime memory for me. Through the years, my escape would grow in importance as I looked back and recalled the details, some better than others, and wondered what life would have been had I never run away from Dad.

I didn't recognize the voices coming from the other room. I was in my bedroom but it didn't really feel like home. We'd spent only a couple of months in this house before the judge had forced me to return to Kansas. The last time I'd slept here was the Sunday after Thanksgiving. The next day, I'd been picked up from school and sent to the detention center.

Mom swung open my door. A woman I'd never seen stood behind her. Mom introduced Nancy Schoessler and her five children, and they all came and stood by my bed. After the intense stress of the past two days, I couldn't handle it and exploded.

Coming into the small house with crooked doors, it was clear that it wasn't as grand as I'd remembered it. I realized this was not going to be easy. And then waking up to this family I didn't know set me off. I was an angry boy. I had first learned that by being mean, you could get your way. Then I learned that if you were angry, you could defend yourself. It was my first way of being. Without Jefferson, I would not have broken that cycle and would not have been able to choose being at peace inside.

"Get out. Get out!" I hollered.

Mom turned pale. The children scattered. Mom looked down at me, and I could see the pain etched on her face.

"So this is the one we've been shedding tears over," Mom's friend said. I had no idea who she was, but she already knew my entire story. The thought infuriated me. She turned and followed her kids out of my room.

I soon realized that Mom's days of keeping secrets were long gone; she had told all our private family matters to the Schoesslers. After years of hiding physical and emotional abuse, she was suddenly willing to share intimate family details with almost anyone. It was a change I found difficult to accept. Still, I regretted my child-scattering outburst almost immediately. Mom and Jefferson had made new friends. I might not know them yet, but these people cared about me. For the first time in years, we didn't need to hide anything. The change came swiftly and dramatically.

"You're going to have to be nicer than that," Mom said. She'd stayed beside my bed when the others left. I wanted to pull my head under the covers and disappear. "A lot of people all over Sequim shed tears for you. They prayed for you."

"Sorry," I said, throwing off my covers.

I smelled bacon sizzling. In the kitchen, I found Jefferson standing at the stove. He wore the same blue overalls he wore every workday. Today, he was cooking bacon and eggs before he left for work. Looking around, I realized the house seemed smaller than I recalled. The red velvet wallpaper and turquoise walls and other decorative touches my mom had made when we moved in were still cheerful, but the rooms felt small. The front porch and utility room was home for Trixie and now also one of her puppies who was blind at birth, Sleepy. There were prune trees in the back, which shaded the small yard. In the front stood the big wood pole barn, unpainted, at least three stories high for stacking and storing hay to feed the dairy cows in winter. The barn overshadowed the little white farmhouse with the turquoise shutters.

Surrounding the Port Williams house and barn were vast green hay fields as far as the eye could see, from all sides. In the distance the Olympic Mountains towered in the south, and to the north flowed the Strait of Juan de Fuca. In the gray morning light, Jefferson finished cooking, and the three of us sat at the kitchen table and ate breakfast together.

Three months earlier we'd eaten Thanksgiving dinner at the same table. As she passed the bacon, Mom told me she and Jefferson had returned to the detention center and brought home Jerry, the American Indian boy who had been there with me. He'd stayed with them about a month before taking off for the reservation again.

I dropped my fork and knife and said, "How could you? How could you substitute another boy for me?"

"We didn't. You told us before you left the detention center that he needed help, so we brought him home."

"What if I came back? I would have had to live with Jerry."

Jefferson said, "It's okay, boy. He ran away again."

I was shocked. I recalled asking them to help him, but I didn't mean for them to bring him home. I felt betrayed and angry. They weren't supposed to replace me while I was gone. It was easy to be furious and resentful about Jerry. After all, he wasn't even nice to me when we were at the detention center. But deep down, I knew Jerry had it worse. He still didn't have a home or a family.

After breakfast, Jefferson went to work. He had taken a job to become a top hand for Maple View Dairy Farm. We had moved into our home at the Maple View Dairy farm, the next farm over from Graysmarsh, just before I had been taken away, so I hadn't had much chance to explore our new surroundings.

I took a walk outside. The Olympic Mountains rose above the lush green foothills. The Strait of Juan de Fuca separated Washington from Canada, and I thought about our ferry ride across the waterway the previous spring and wondered what would happen next. Would the judge send me back to Kansas yet again? Would I be allowed to stay with Mom and Jefferson? Would I ever get to live without worrying? Was it risky to get attached to this place once again?

I learned more about Mom and Jefferson's legal fight during my first days back in Sequim. A state appeals court had determined that the Kansas order giving Dad custody was unsupported by fact. According to the new ruling, the Kansas court failed to show any misconduct by Mom but instead made vague references to "*her association with Black people.*" So on January 14, 1971, while I languished at Tall Oaks, the Court of Appeals of the State of Washington reversed the order sending me back to Kansas. There was just one little problem, as I'd found out: The ruling held no weight, at least not in Kansas. Its enforceability required my presence in Washington, which meant my running away was not only full of risk but also legal. At least, that's the way I looked at it. I never worried about seeing my dad again. My parents, especially my dad, had forced me to make a choice. I never looked back.

It also meant something else. Dad had kept custody of me in direct violation of the Washington State order. Even if he didn't need to abide by it, he certainly didn't tell me about it. In part, that explained why it was so important for him to intercept my mail. Had I learned about the appeals court's decision, I almost certainly would have done everything I could to get back to Sequim. As it turned out, all Dad needed to do to push me over the edge was tackle and punch me.

Back in Sequim, additional hearings would be held to determine my fate. Although the appeals court ruled in favor of Mom and Jefferson, it also ordered further litigation. In the meantime, I reenrolled at Sequim Middle School. My classmates were shocked. Many of them had last seen me through the bulletproof glass of a police car, driving away from campus. In some ways, my return also surprised me. Looking out the patrol car window three months earlier, I didn't know if I'd ever see this place again. Now that I was back, school seemed the least of my concerns.

When Mom told me a trial date had been set, I was elated. The trial opened on Tuesday March 9, 1971. Brooke Taylor continued to serve as our attorney. For the first time I'd be allowed to testify, and I took off from school on Monday to prepare. My excitement soon waned. The judge heard testimony from two out-of-town witnesses who traveled to Sequim on our behalf. Grandma Hughes and Esther, a close friend of Mom's, were the only two allowed to take the stand. Esther would become an on-and-off-again lifelong friend and companion to Mom. After Esther graduated from high school, she started her own beauty school in Bonner Springs where I would take my mom weekly to get her hair done. Esther always worried me because she smoked and didn't seem to be a good influence on my mom. But, again, she was another safe haven.

Esther told the court that Dad regularly called Mom "a bitch or a whore." She also recalled the day Mom and I moved out of Tall Oaks. Esther had come over to help, and Dad stormed into the room and said Mom didn't need her. Then he turned to Esther and said, "Let me tell you one thing. What she needs is one last beating, and I'm going to give it to her if it's the last thing I do. She's going to be miserable the rest of her life."

Her testimony shocked me. I'd seen Dad hit Mom many times, but I never heard him speak like that. Esther also recalled how Mom would come to her house late at night. She described bite marks covering Mom's body and bruises on her neck. The worst time, she said, was when Mom had knife marks on her neck.

It was Esther's house that Mom had run to all those nights when I'd awakened to the sounds of violence. She often arrived at Esther's home in tears. Looking back, I don't think I realized how bad the abuse had become. The thought of Dad holding a knife to Mom's throat brought me to tears. Mom and I had talked a bit about the abuse after their divorce when we lived by ourselves, but she never went into detail with me. She simply reached a point where she couldn't stand my father's meanness any longer, so she left. She never dwelled on it and did not exactly think of herself as an abused woman. She felt they just couldn't live together because they were such different people, and she believed it was partly her fault. For years she had thought that she was supposed to stay because marriage vows were for life, and her parents never encouraged her to leave. Finally, she left because she understood that it was never going to get any better. She had to leave to survive.

During the two months I was back in Tall Oaks with Dad, Esther had tried to visit me five or six times. Dad never let her come close. Once, she knocked on the door at Tall Oaks and Dad verbally assaulted her, telling her she had no business coming around and claiming she was in a gang. Then he warned her to keep away.

Esther knew how bad things were between Dad and me. A few years earlier, she had witnessed an extreme emotional breakdown of mine following a weekend with Dad. When Mom couldn't calm me down, she called a doctor who gave me some medicine to relax.

Esther had also witnessed one of my recurring nightmares. Just before her testimony, she stayed with us in Sequim. That night I woke up screaming: "Don't let him take me! Don't let him take me! He'll get me." In the dream, I was looking out my bedroom window at Tall Oaks as Mom's Volkswagen bug sped away down the long gravel driveway; simultaneously, Dad pounded at the door, coming after Mom. His anger had reached across my bedroom, across the trundle bed, and out the window to snatch Mom out of the VW. I could never tell if she had gotten away, but the dream would almost always end with me shouting, "Take me with you!"

Grandma Hughes also testified about Dad's abuse and about my fear. She recalled watching Dad punch Mom and seeing bruises on Mom during her pregnancy. She said Dad had warned her to stay away when I was back at Tall Oaks. Once, he let me write a letter inviting my grandparents to visit. In the same envelope, Grandma said, Dad put a second letter. It told them not to come.

———————

Grandma and Esther returned home to the Midwest shortly after their testimony. The rest of us didn't return to court until late July. During this time I remained with Mom and Jefferson in Sequim. With each passing month it began to feel more like home. Jefferson began to reemerge as a preacher. He held a sunrise Easter service for a small group at Port Williams and regular Sunday services at American Legion Post 62.

As I settled back into life in Sequim, I realized something for the first time: We were poor. Near the end of the school year, when I was thirteen, Mom and Jefferson encouraged me to find a summer job. We needed the extra money. Mom didn't work, and Jefferson held a low-wage job with little opportunity for advancement. Mom motivated me by pointing out that I could pick berries if I didn't find anything else. The only problem was that jobs available to a thirteen-year-old were limited, even in a farming community.

I found my salvation at a local oyster farm. I worked early mornings on the tide flats. I'd been mesmerized by the Strait of Juan de Fuca since we arrived on the Olympic Peninsula. When I learned about the oyster job, it sounded perfect. I spent most mornings tending the flats, pulling large sacks from shallow water, placing mature oysters in huge buckets, seeding new beds, and otherwise helping out. If a menial task needed doing, I did it. And I loved every minute of it. Standing on the water, I could look north toward Canada and south at the snow-capped Olympic Mountains. In the morning light, it was hard to imagine a better place anywhere.

Jefferson left for work every weekday morning before five o'clock. Later, he also took a night job cleaning the Dungeness Inn. For his sermons at the Sequim American Legion Post 62 Jefferson made a pulpit out of plywood, and the small group that attended sat on folding chairs. Mom played piano. I had practically forgotten she knew how.

Word about Jefferson's preaching and singing spread slowly through Sequim. As we met more and more people, there was greater risk of being found.

My final custody hearing took place on July 29, 1971. The courthouse on Lincoln Street in Port Angeles stood just a few blocks from where Mom, Jefferson, and I spent our first night on the Olympic Peninsula. The historic brick building impressed and frightened me at the same time. I knew that whatever the judge decided would be final.

Mom, Jefferson, and I entered the courtroom together. Dark wooden bench seats with high backs filled most of the room. A line of windows running along the south wall admitted bright light from outside. Two banisters separated the front of the room from the rest,

Port Williams

and two tables sat opposite each other in front of the judge's bench with a space mimicking an aisle between them.

I sat in front on one side with Mom and Jefferson. Dad sat with his attorney at the table across from us. Two large flags—the Stars and Stripes and the green Washington State flag with a picture of George Washington—bracketed the judge's bench. The same dark wood that paneled the bench seats behind us also decorated the judge's bench and the wall behind him. The wall's heavy varnish reflected the light from outside.

Some of the members of Jefferson's church filed into the public viewing area. So did others from the Sequim community. Looking behind us, I saw some of my classmates and their families.

As the proceedings began, part of me wanted to stand up and tell everyone about Dad's abuse—about how he'd beaten Mom, about how I watched him strangle her, hit her, and throw her to the ground. Memories rushed over me, and I couldn't help but think about the old house in Edwardsville. For a moment, I forgot about the violence and saw myself standing in the front yard after a snowstorm. It always seemed so peaceful right after a fresh snow, surrounded by whiteness and quiet in the gap of silence between passing trains. As a little boy, never did I feel as safe as when I went outside to play in the snow.

The hearing lasted two days. Dad's attorney argued that Jefferson was unfit to raise me. Rather than base his case on race—we weren't in Kansas anymore, after all—he argued that Jefferson's lack of a high school diploma made him unfit to be a father. He also dug up old rumors about Mom having a romantic relationship with a Black student at Bonner Springs High.

The judge accepted witness testimony given in Kansas. A handful of people spoke on Dad's behalf. Each talked about his strong community standing, his skills as a pastor, and his leadership as a camp counselor. One of the witnesses had attended Phillips University with Mom and Dad. Another met them shortly after we moved to Edwardsville. One of them called Mom a "controversial woman" and said she "would give special attention to colored children and carry on with them." Another witness said Mom was responsible for the "weakening of the faith of a great many people."

Brooke Taylor fought back with witnesses who spoke about Dad's abuse and about my fear of my father. He also called on Sequim community members, who talked about our family and about Jefferson's paternal character. On the second day of the hearing, the judge called me to the stand. For the first time in fourteen years, I spoke openly and on the record about the abuse I'd grown up with.

At one point, he asked the question I had long wanted to answer in front of a judge. "Who do you want to live with, Scottie?"

I didn't hesitate. "My mom and Jefferson."

Dad stared at me from a few feet away.

Before I stepped down, I made one final plea: "Please don't send me back to Kansas."

My time on the stand passed quickly. The courtroom remained silent as I stepped down and sat beside Mom and Jefferson. Shortly afterward, the judge dismissed us. Before he did, he said he'd review the evidence and testimony and make his decision in a few days.

I was shocked. What else did he need to hear? Why couldn't he just say we won and send Dad back to Kansas? I walked out of the courtroom feeling uneasy. Dad approached me in the hallway. I began to tremble as he spoke.

"No matter what happens, I want you to know I love you," he said.

I froze. We hadn't talked since the night I ran away. I couldn't remember ever hearing him say those words before. I didn't know what to do. Before I could speak, Mom stepped to my side, said goodbye, and led me down the hall.

On August 6, 1971, Judge Joseph H. Johnston awarded my care, custody, and control to Mom. In addition, the court recognized my affection for Jefferson and noted that he, Mom, and I shared "a relationship of mutual affection, trust, and respect."

The judge noted my fear of my father and called out the Kansas court for taking me away from Mom without reason. Then, citing geographical reality and our deteriorating relationship, the judge stripped Dad of all legal visitation rights. He assigned a mediator to help us discuss the possibility of future visits, but neither one of us ever followed up.

In the four decades since Judge Johnston's decision, I have many times wondered how my life would have turned out had he ruled the other way.

During the rest of my time in Sequim, Dad never called or wrote a letter to me. Three and a half years after the custody ruling, Jefferson and I returned to the courthouse and changed my legal name to Scott Jackson. I never called my biological father "Dad" again.

By September of 1972, Jefferson's little congregation at the American Legion post was flourishing. When a local Methodist church put its building up for sale, Jefferson's parishioners pooled fifteen hundred dollars and bought it. They called it the Little Brown Church of Blyn, taking the title from the song "The Church in the Wildwood."

The building was one room with a small walled-off kitchen. As the congregation grew, we added extensions for Sunday school and social events. The church thrived in those early years. Jefferson never accepted a salary, and he never wrote a sermon. He preached the words God gave him, and he never ran out of things to say. His most popular sermon each year came on Easter when the congregation and a large number of guests gathered at the beach at nearby Port Williams. Jefferson saw Easter as an opportunity to baptize as many people as he could in the cold saltwater. I recall standing on the sand and watching him dunk newcomers while he stood waist deep off the beach in the morning light.

We also hosted an annual pig roast. Each summer, we buried a pig and let it cook through the night. The following day, always a Sunday, we dug up the meat after church. Christian or not, people came from all around to taste that pork, considered by many to be the Olympic Peninsula's best.

Our live nativity scene also brought the crowds. Each year, we welcomed live farm animals to the property in front of the church. Adults and children from the congregation joined them in an impressive re-creation of the first Christmas. Mom spent each fall sewing costumes for everyone who participated, including me. The best years were those when a new baby joined the congregation, giving us a live actor for the role of baby Jesus.

If Jefferson was the Little Brown Church's shepherd, Mom was its leading lady, musical influence, and lead social planner. Much like she had done back in Edwardsville, she embraced her role as pastor's wife. She played the piano each Sunday, helped anyone who needed it, and made sure no church event lacked a proper celebration, however big or small.

Reverend Pat Wright began to bring her Total Experience Children's Choir from Seattle to the Little Brown Church. Wright had arrived in Seattle in 1974 and grown into the city's first lady of gospel music. The Little Brown Church was the first place she brought the choir outside of Seattle so they could sing with Jefferson. There was always a packed church when they visited. Soon after, the rumors started to fly. The Sequim townspeople worried that Blacks from the Seattle central district were going to move over and camp out on the Little Brown Church grounds. Fortunately, that rumor finally got squashed.

Our family was always a novelty. Jefferson embraced it. He met every store owner, every waitress, every child, all with a smile. There was no one he met that he didn't like. In turn, they had to like Jefferson. He was a farmer just like them. The Pacific Northwest was different. Vancouver, British Columbia, was an especially international community—there just weren't many African Americans. But we couldn't stay in Vancouver. In Port Angeles, there were difficulties with getting a taxi or a hotel room and plenty of stares. But from the day we drove the Studebaker to Sequim, it was a more accepting place.

The man on the Coho Ferry was right—people from all over the world were settling in Sequim. Yes, it was the beginning of the retirees' influx, but also writers, artists, and hippies were all mixing with traditional dairy farmers and the berry farmers, which predated today's lavender farms. Still, other than the Schoessler family, we didn't receive many invitations to dinner from anyone in Sequim. Jefferson never showed it, but he knew what I knew—that there were some places neither he nor our family would be invited.

Jefferson's preaching and singing continued to inspire me as much as they had that first day back at Gethsemane Baptist. As we continued to make ourselves a home in Sequim, nowhere did I feel more at peace than sitting in the pews of the Little Brown Church.

The first couple of years back in Sequim were not always easy for me. I spent a good part of the time testing my mom and Jefferson. I questioned school; I questioned the two of them. I angrily questioned Jefferson and sometimes challenged his authority. But the few times that I tried to take out our circumstances on my mom, Jefferson would intervene. One of our worst experiences was when I talked back to my mom, and he asked me to stop. I wouldn't, and we wound up wrestling through the kitchen. I said words I shouldn't have. Jefferson smacked me across the cheek or shoulder, but it was more about getting me to shut up. He was so strong that he knocked me across the room into my drum set. Whenever he would tell me to stop talking back or yelling at my mom, I would then react to him.

"Boy, you got to stop talking back to your mom and be nice to her."

"But she isn't nice to me."

"It doesn't matter, Boy. She's your mom and you are the child, so you have to obey her."

"But she's wrong."

"It doesn't matter. Boy, I don't care what you call me, but you are not going to call your mother names in front of me."

During this time I also struggled to find my way in school, but Jefferson encouraged me. I remember sitting at our little kitchen table at night. The room's single overhead lamp cast a yellow circle of light on my homework. Jefferson sat with me, doing his best, with his limited education, to help me.

One afternoon I accidentally let the pig out of the pen. Jefferson took his shotgun outside and fired it into the air, just meaning to scare the pig. We all watched it fall dead. My mom was so angry and in tears at the same time. She started screaming at Jefferson. This time, he'd had enough. Mom kept screaming and he finally just walked out of the house, climbed into his green Dodge truck, and drove away. He didn't come back for hours.

Mom and I began to wonder if he would ever return. We couldn't blame him. After all, although a terrible thing had happened, there were a lot more important things in our life than the loss of the pig. After dark, Jefferson made his way back. He didn't come inside; he made a fire outside near the pole barn and heated some water. He dressed the pig and I went and watched him. Mom came out and joined us. We had survived together, and it didn't make sense to fall apart now. That night, I understood some of the sacrifices that Jefferson had made to be here in Sequim, without his extended family, without anyone else he knew—just to be with the two of us.

Jefferson and I became closer during these years, too. When I began to question my faith and Christianity during high school, Jefferson supported my searching. He listened patiently and encouraged me as I read other religious works, including sections of the Koran and writings about the Kabbalah. Through it all, Jefferson pointed to what he saw as Christianity's two most important principles: forgiveness and redemption.

We often had conversations in the evening around nine or ten o'clock, when we would be in the kitchen together. I would just be getting to my homework, and he would be getting ready to go to bed.

"Jefferson, I've now read the Koran, and I've studied Buddhism and Hinduism, and read the Bible all the way through, and I still believe in God. But what I don't know is what's different about the Christian faith compared to all these other faiths. They also seem important, so why Christianity instead of these other faiths?"

"Boy, none of those faiths are bad. It's more important how you live your life. Even people without faith can live a godly life just by being good to others. The reason I believe in Christianity is because we can all be forgiven no matter what we've done, and I'm not perfect."

These conversations were as much about forgiving myself as accepting my faith. I always thought that I was less than perfect, that I wasn't worthy. Because of the way I grew up, maybe my mom and I had done something to deserve all this. I never really forgave myself. But through Jefferson, I began to see that I was worthy and, more important, could choose to do something meaningful with my life.

CHAPTER SEVEN

Making My Way

Not long after the final custody trial, Mom and Jefferson announced their plan to adopt a child. I was shocked and a little jealous after everything we had been through. For the first time in years, I felt like everything was going great. Why in the world would they want another child? More selfishly, why didn't they want to focus on me? After all, it was hard enough. We were poor.

They applied for adoption through the state foster care system and requested a newborn of mixed race. There was no financial cost, and they didn't have to wait long since they were an interracial couple who wanted a mixed-race child. When the news came a few months later, it seemed like a dream. Somewhere in Eastern Washington in the city of Spokane—which seemed just as unfamiliar as Sequim did when we first arrived there—seven hours away, a little girl was waiting for her new parents. Mom and Jefferson left the next day by bus. When they returned two days later, I was a big brother. I had used part of my paycheck to pay for a white snowsuit for the baby, and they brought her home in it.

They introduced me to Jeffie-Lou Jackson, named after Jefferson and Sydney-Lou. I thought, *Who in the world would name their daughter Jeffie-Lou?* Nonetheless, it was one of the happiest days of my life. I fell in love with my little sister the moment I saw her. She was a cherub, with fat dimpled cheeks on both sides. Mom dressed her in a blue

Shawne and Jeffie-Lou

bonnet. She wasn't happy about it either. Her skin was a beautiful shade of mocha, and she had dark brown soft loose curls everywhere. I loved her at first sight.

Thanks to mom's sewing, taste, and style, Jeffie-Lou grew up the most boldly dressed child on our side of Puget Sound. She quickly became the center of our world. She was dynamic and beautiful, and she filled our home with a new sense of joy and purpose. Then came another surprise. A few months after Jeffie-Lou joined our family, we received a call. Shawne Hosea was three years old. He had already been through seven foster homes and now needed a new place to live. Like Jeffie-Lou, he was of mixed race. Several families had wanted to adopt him but couldn't afford his medical bills. Shawne had severe allergies and asthma and required an expensive regimen of cortisone medication. He joined our family as a foster child. That was the only way the state would pay his medical expenses. For Mom and Jefferson, that wasn't good enough.

When Mom read a news story about a doctor in Seattle who had experienced a similar issue and was awarded medical support from the legislature, she sped into action. An occasional parishioner from the Little Brown Church served in state government as our state legislator and helped Mom learn more. After many phone calls and a stack of paperwork, we were accepted into the new program. We adopted Shawne soon afterward.

Shawne and I shared a bedroom. At night, he'd wake up screaming and gasping for air. I'd rush to his side to help. Many times, I thought we were going to lose him. As his medical problems continued, so did our worries. I learned to stay up late and operate on a few hours of sleep. It was the best way to make sure I would be ready if anything went wrong. Perhaps in helping to take care of Shawne and Jeffie-Lou, I learned to put aside myself in favor of others.

Mom tried desperately to improve Shawne's health. She altered his diet, changed his medicines, and threw away everything she thought might cause an allergic reaction. She made sure his inhalers and prescriptions were close at all times. We even sent him to Denver, when he was older, to see the top respiratory doctors in the country. By the time he left, doctors said he was likely getting as good care at home as he could in a hospital.

Mom encouraged me to take a speech class my first year in high school. She then helped me write speeches and with the support of the Speech and Debate Club coach, who believed I had potential, I began to win every competition. Grandma Hughes was proud too, even if my speeches weren't sermons. My specialty was like a sermon—the long oratory. It had to be ten minutes long, recited from memory, and an original work. After school, when no one was around, I would stand in front of the only full-length mirror in our little house and practice my oration and delivery. Sometimes, I would catch myself embracing the words and other times, I would imagine, as I looked into the mirror, that my words would have an impact on others.

The speech that took me all the way to the state championship was about bondage and prejudice. I started it by singing a few lines of the Russian slave song, "Yo, heave ho!" I was awarded first place in the regional competition, and my coach and I were the only ones from Sequim traveling across the state to Ellensburg for the Washington State Speech and Debate Competition. I remember the coach driving down Highway 101 on the descent to the Hood Canal Bridge. You could see the Olympic Mountains and the sparkling blue water of Hood Canal. I knew I was supposed to be here.

After each round, my name was called to compete in the next round. Then the final round arrived. We didn't know what to think. The other two students had done a great job, and I had done my best, delivering my speech flawlessly. When the time came for them to announce the State Champion in each category, they saved oratory for last. Sure enough, they called my name. Sequim High School displayed my trophy. It was amazing. The very issue that had brought me to Sequim and turned our lives upside down was now the subject of my winning oratory: "No one should be kept from realizing their full potential because of the limitations of others." When we returned to Sequim, it was past midnight. I woke up my parents. They weren't as excited to be awakened as I was to tell them the news. Regardless, it was a great accomplishment.

I became more confident in myself. I was starting to enjoy school and excel in my schoolwork. I even wanted to play sports, especially basketball, but instead I applied for a job at Southwoods, the Sequim Country dry goods store, and was hired. I needed my after-school job. It gave me independence. Some weeks, I earned as much money as my parents did. Southwoods was owned by Chuck and Howard. Many in Sequim said they were a couple, but they were my friends and mentors, and I didn't care. They taught me how to eat escargot and made sure I had nice clothes to wear. They also owned the Town and Country clothing store across the street from Southwoods, and sometimes they would have me model the clothes for the local newspaper ads.

Working there wasn't always fun and games. There were fourteen older women who served as clerks under Chuck and Howard. At first I thought I knew it all, especially how to sweep the floors and take out the trash. I would do everything as quickly as I could, not paying attention that I wasn't always taking the time to do a good job. The clerks started complaining that I was too sloppy and careless, quick to get the job done but not careful enough to do it well. Chuck and Howard would not have this. One evening, they took me aside and let me know that they would have to fire me if I didn't learn to do a complete job. I was caught off guard, but I learned quickly a deeper sense of humility. I learned to do my best regardless of the task. I soon became the best sweeper of floors and even cleaned the toilets, and the clerks never complained again. Instead they finally got together with Chuck and Howard and welcomed me into the Southwoods close-knit family.

During my junior year of high school, my peers started calling me "Action Jackson" and elected me student body president. Just as I was finally feeling accepted and like I belonged, my mother pushed me out of my comfort zone and insisted that I apply for a Rotary international exchange program. She felt strongly—much more than I did—that if I got the chance to travel as an international exchange student, it would be the experience of a lifetime. She knew that I was young for my class, so it wouldn't hurt to enter college a year later. She also understood that we didn't necessarily have the means for me to attend college. After the interviews, I didn't think much more about the application. Then, one dark, wet, and cold December evening, Mom and I arrived home at the same time, and she picked up the mail from the mailbox and followed me in the door near the plum trees.

"Scottie," she leaped, "you got it! You've been accepted as a Rotary exchange student to New Zealand."

"What? When?" I asked, not even hearing or caring about the choice of country. "When do they want me to go?" I repeated.

"They want you to leave January 12th in time for the beginning of the school year Down Under."

There was a sinking feeling in my stomach.

"I can't go," I blurted out.

"You can't *not* go," she replied. My mom was emphatic. "You are not going to lose the chance of a lifetime to see the world."

"We'll see," I said. "I told them on the application I couldn't go until after the school year. Maybe I could appeal."

But Rotary only had the one placement. I had to take the opportunity or give it to the next student. Jefferson thought I should go, but not as strongly as Mom. Everyone at school thought I should go, even the teachers, and especially the principal as he was a Rotarian and had been my sponsor for the application. *But what about graduation?* I thought. I couldn't bear the thought of coming back and having to go through one more semester to graduate. I wouldn't be student body president and the few friends I had would be gone. I only had one class left: American history.

The teachers devised a plan whereby if I read the textbook and then successfully passed both a written and oral exam, I would be allowed to graduate in absentia with my class.

Even Howard and Chuck of Southwoods agreed that I should go. They bought my luggage and made sure that I had new clothes to take with me. I passed the exams, packed my bags, and said my goodbyes. Suddenly, I was headed to New Zealand whether I wanted to or not.

I left in January, reluctantly, abdicating my position as student body president and finishing my high school degree six months early. The Sunday before I left, I sat in the front of the Little Brown Church

and listened to Jefferson preach. I remember the congregation singing "Love Lifted Me." The refrain struck me as particularly beautiful on this day.

> *Love lifted me!*
> *Love lifted me!*
> *When nothing else could help,*
> *Love lifted me!*

The sun seemed to shine brighter than usual for January. I remember how warm it felt on my arm through the church windows. Jefferson was preaching with extra emotion. Mom played the piano, and
Jeffie-Lou and Shawne, my adopted sister and brother, sat next to me
in the front pew. The church was packed. Jefferson always preached
from scripture. I especially liked to hear him preach on the 23rd
Psalm. The words came to him with ease.

> *The Lord is my shepherd, I shall not be in want.*
> *He makes me lie down in green pastures,*
> *He leads me beside quiet waters,*
> *He restores my soul.*

Listening to him, I thought about everything we had been
through since that day we first met at Gethsemane Baptist. As the
service winded down, Jefferson looked right at me.

"This is a special day," he said. "Scottie, our number one son, is
leaving tomorrow. Come up here, son. We are all very proud of you."

I didn't want to go away again, even to New Zealand. I was just learning how to belong. As Jefferson spoke of how proud he was, I thought,
Don't they want me here? Why is everyone so happy I'm leaving?

I had no idea this was going to happen.

"We want you to say a few words before you go."

I didn't know what to say, so I spoke from the heart.

"Thank you. You all have meant everything to me. When we arrived in Sequim, we didn't know anyone. Now I feel like I'm leaving behind more than I could ever have imagined. You stood beside us when it mattered most. Without you, the Little Brown Church, and your faith in me and my family, none of this would have been possible."

When I started to walk back down from the pulpit to the pew, Mom spoke up. "Scottie, we want you to play our song."

I returned to the piano. My mother loved this song because I had written it for her when just the two of us had lived in our trailer on the Edwardsville farm. I had written it from the heart and to avoid piano practice. I began to play. There were many chords in my song, and then I started to sing.

When I was little, my mother used to sit me on her lap.
She would read me the stories of the Bible and I used to love
them so very much.

Six months later, my parents called long distance to New Zealand to report that Jefferson had been asked to give the high school graduation invocation and receive my diploma. It was the only high school diploma Jefferson would ever receive, even if it was mine.

Jefferson had never received a high school diploma because he had left school to work full time on the farm before he finished the tenth grade, at least two years short of being able to graduate. So when he was asked to give the invocation for the Sequim High School graduation that year and receive my diploma in my absence, it was a big deal.

Afterward people in Sequim said it was one of the most meaningful invocations ever at graduation. Jefferson of course was the only person of color either on stage or in the audience. But we were used to that by now. Knowing that Jefferson and Mom were there, even though I wasn't, made it seem a little better. Jefferson was proud of me and I was proud of him. I was thousands of miles away in New Zealand, but we were still connected. In fact, I always felt connected to Jefferson no matter what the circumstances. It was something I could count on and perhaps a feeling I only had with two other people—but in different ways—Mom and Grandpa Whitey.

———————

My year in New Zealand introduced me to the world and left a lasting impression on me. New Zealanders talked funny and drove on the wrong side of the road. We wore uniforms to school. I went to Rotary meetings every week, which always started with everyone standing and singing "God Save the Queen." I lived with four different host families, including a Maori family. The Maori people of Polynesian descent were the first people to inhabit New Zealand. I recognized for the first time that the gap between rich and poor didn't just exist in the United States but around the world. I learned there are good people everywhere in the world regardless of race, religion, or culture, willing to help others.

In New Zealand I was another white person in a predominately white society. It was easy to fit in. But when I lived with my Maori host family, I was reminded once again of the impact of race. My Maori mother watched over me and even taught me how to drive on the wrong side of the road, until we both learned that Rotary had an international policy prohibiting exchange students from driving. One day my Maori host father informed me that his sister had died, and that he wanted me to come with them to the family wake.

The wake lasted three days and was held in a long house where we mourned with the body. The front entrance to the long house was decorated in Maori traditional motif with a very small opening. Statuesque totem poles surrounded the house, which had a series of masks carved into the wood. The roofline was an A-frame with beams pointing down, and the roof boards had the classic Polynesian curved motif. We had to stoop down to get inside, but then we were able to stand up again. Once we entered, it was clear that the structure extended back considerably. On each side of the house was a long, built-in bench with carvings on both sides. Each side of the house had cots and mats where we would sleep. The body was placed at the far end in an open casket like a shroud in a wooden holder, resembling a manger.

Mid-morning of the third and final day, we left the long house and walked across the gravel road to the local pub. At first, it was only the mourning party, and I was the only nonfamily member. Then the community members began to filter into the pub and join the cele-bration. Tables started to fill; bar stools had people sitting two and three deep. The air was filled with a mixture of laughter, tears, and memories. The bar served draft and tap beer at room temperature. We slept in the long house again that night. After a final full day and night of celebration for a woman I had met only after she died, the casket was finally closed and my Maori host father's sister could now rest in peace.

My Maori host family in New Zealand was not like my other host families. My host brother was very smart but didn't have the same opportunities as the other brothers and sisters in the other families. As a Maori family, they also suffered every day in some way from sys-temic racism and from prejudice in some form by the white majority in the country. But like Jefferson, my Maori mom and dad chose the positive in their lives regardless of circumstances. There was a lot of love in the Maori culture—unconditional love—and it reminded me of the unconditional love of Jefferson and his family.

My year Down Under came to an end too quickly. What remained were a broader point of view and a greater understanding of cultural differences and perspectives. For the first time, I understood that there were kids like me around the world who experienced similar preju-dices and struggles.

I went home to face the challenges of being in Sequim and to find my way forward.

The log cabin

While I was away in New Zealand, Jefferson and Mom bought five
acres in the woods. After picking me up from the Seattle airport, we
returned to the log cabin they had literally built with their own hands.
Two stained glass windows with the words "God is Love" and "Love
Thy Neighbor" reflected the labor of love it took to build the cabin.
The cabin was deep in the woods, halfway up Lost Mountain Road.

As I walked up to the cabin for the first time, I couldn't help but
be amazed. It was a remarkable sight. The cedar logs had come from
the property and had been milled nearby at one of the portable mills
in the area. This is where they smoothed the two sides of the log that
would be stacked atop each other and left the rounded sides for facing inside and outside. The cabin was huge and even larger once you
were inside. Jefferson had taken a string to measure how large the
cabin would be, and he kept expanding the string, not sure it looked
big enough.

It was an open loft design. The bedrooms were all on the loft
level, except for the one guest bedroom. There were no doors to the

bedrooms. The balcony railing separated the bedrooms from the expansive first floor below. The railing and the stairs leading to the second level loft were made from the same rough-cut logs milled from the property. The ceiling was thirty feet high, which added to the sense of expansiveness when you looked down from the balcony to the kitchen, dining room, and living room. Those rooms were appointed with faux oriental rugs over the Douglas fir planks that made up the floor. Antique wood stoves were placed throughout the cabin. A paper maché zebra nestled in one corner, Mother's colorful hats and dolls in another. The sixteen-foot-high china cabinet Mom bought with my tax return from working at Southwoods while I was in New Zealand was in another corner.

Sydney and Jefferson had made a home that was uniquely ours. They explained they had made sure to carefully place letters they had received from me when I was taken back to Kansas along with a picture of me in a small memory box that was under the cornerstone of the cabin. In this way, the reasons why we were here amongst the cedar and fir trees would never be forgotten. The Schoesslers gave us a North American Chestnut tree, which was carefully planted in the front yard.

The log cabin served as yet another anchor, together with the Little Brown Church, to remind me that we had found a home. I was in awe of what Mom and Jefferson had accomplished in a year while I was gone. I was also afraid that after all I had achieved before I had left for the exchange year, I was back to where I started—without a foreseeable future.

Where Are
the Scholarships?

I was was determined to go to an Ivy League school—or at least one with ivy-covered brick buildings. My mom was more realistic and encouraged me to work and attend a nearby community college. Despite my success as an international student, I returned from New Zealand without a single college scholarship. I had spent hours completing applications before I left, but Mom told me she had never mailed any of them, including the final submissions to Harvard and the University of Chicago, where I was pursuing small school talent criteria. Mom explained that we couldn't afford the difference in what we would still have had to pay for tuition even with financial aid. I was devastated. For the first time in my life, I felt like she had let me down.

I truly thought life would be easier when I returned home to Sequim after my year in New Zealand. Wasn't everything supposed to fall into place? I didn't understand why Sydney had not kept the application process going for colleges. I didn't understand why she had spent my savings, including a tax refund, on a china cabinet. I felt like I was in a bigger hole than ever, with no job, no car, no scholarship opportunities, and no colleges to go to, or so it seemed. I was angry about those things. But then I realized that it probably wasn't the china cabinet she had spent the money on. That was just a cover-up. More likely it was groceries. Sydney and Jefferson were still there supporting me. I recognized in those first few weeks that nothing was going to come easily. The attention of being an exchange student was gone. My anger began to dissipate, and there was more room for resolve. It would be up to me to find a job, save money, and apply and get accepted to a college. Having the opportunity to be an exchange student didn't change any of that. It just seemed like a big mountain to climb.

Instead of the Ivy League, I found a job at a nearby plywood mill to save for a more substantial school. Howard and Chuck were willing to let me work at Southwoods again, but I wouldn't earn enough there to pay for a four-year college. They then used their connections to get me an interview for a position at the Port Angeles Plywood Mill. The work was hard, and they normally hired older people, but I managed to get a position. There were some college students who worked at the plywood mill in the summers. But this was February, the dead of winter. It was mainly men and women, some in their twenties and thirties but many much older, who worked there and counted it as their livelihood. They would work there the rest of their adult lives, if they were lucky and the mill continued to operate.

The plywood mill was located fifteen miles away on the other side of Port Angeles, near the water. The steam rose from the plywood kilns twenty-four hours a day. The work was some of the hardest I had ever done. It was physical, hot, and tedious, pushing wet, heavy veneer into a large dryer half the size of a football field. Then there was stocking the dry sheets of plywood, and even harder the cleanup detail—lifting the endless Brenner scraps into carts and taking them to the incinerators.

It was shift work—eight hours, twelve hours, or even sometimes a double shift of sixteen hours, which also meant getting paid time and a half. I joined the union of the International Woodworkers of America and got to know some interesting men and women, including former members of the sometimes controversial Industrial Workers of the World—the "Wobblies" as they were commonly known in earlier days of the labor movement.

Everyone got paid a good living wage, which is why they worked there. At first I thought there was no meaning in the work, and I was frustrated and impatient that this was my best chance to earn enough money to go to college. I couldn't count on scholarships. Days turned into weeks and then months, sometimes 16-hour days when I could get double shifts.

Over the months I realized that each of the men and women who worked at the Plywood Mill had their own worth and their own story. Like Jefferson, they did manual labor so they could provide for their families, send their kids to college, and live in one of the most beautiful places in the world—the Olympic Peninsula.

I soon became a favorite for taking on extra shifts. They knew I was trying to make as much money as possible. I would work Saturday shifts and double shifts whenever someone didn't show for work or got sick or was on vacation. I started to listen more to my coworkers in the break room. We got a half hour for lunch and two 15-minute breaks; they were mandatory union rules. They had their own stories and wisdom, each of them. There was often wisdom in their words about whatever the subject might be. Like Jefferson, they had lived and knew a lot more about everyday life than I did.

I also began to take pride in the Union IWA of which I was now a member and in the product—plywood—we created and produced at the mill. After all, it was a big part of what we use to build our homes. This was the Pacific Northwest, and I was a part of the wood products industry where Douglas Fir and Cedar surrounded us, growing like grass reaching up into the sky on the hillside of the Olympic Mountains. I would eventually come back on holidays and summers during college.

The mill work was never easy, but understanding and learning more about the men and women who worked at the mill did become easier. There were different jobs: pushing the wet layers or sheets into the kilns that together made up a larger sheet of plywood, or working the receiving end, taking the finished plywood out of the kilns, now much heavier, and stacking it for further drying and sorting. My favorite assignment was working in the chip tower where I would shovel the wood chips used to fuel the steam-powered kilns. It was hard work but considered one of the more prestigious jobs at the mill, partly because it was hard manual labor. It paid 50 cents more per hour as well. The rich and poignant smell of burning wood and freshly cut wood chips permeated everything, including my clothes.

But I still had to contribute to room and board at home because my parents didn't make much money and struggled financially, and working at the mill did not cover my expenses and enable me to save for college. Unless I was working the all-night shift at the mill, I was expected to accompany Jefferson each night from just after midnight to 5:00 a.m. to clean the Dungeness Inn Golf Course Restaurant and Banquet Center. I would vacuum and then clean the toilets and the bathrooms on all three floors. Jefferson would clean the kitchen, including the hard work of cleaning the grease-caked commercial grills. Then he would mop the kitchen floors. If I finished before Jefferson, I would either play the piano downstairs in the banquet room or lie down on the banquet room carpet and take a nap. When Jefferson finished first, he would sometimes make us both a ham and cheese deli sandwich and pour a soda from the fountain machine before we would make our way back up the mountain to the log cabin. I generally slept in a couple of two-hour increments, between 10:00 p.m. and 12:00 a.m. and then again between 5:00 a.m. and 7:00 a.m.

The drive to the Dungeness Inn in Jefferson's precious green Dodge pickup truck, which by now was beginning to show signs of age, never seemed so hard because we would leave around midnight, and I did better late at night. In fact, sometimes I was lucky to get home in time to leave with him. But the ride home at five in the morning was always harder for me. Most mornings on the way home, we didn't say much to each other. But there were mornings when a cougar would cross the road. Or we might see a deer. One morning, Jefferson told me he knew growing up like this wasn't always easy.

"Boy, I know it isn't easy being my number one son and having to work to help out the family," he said.

"I don't mind," I replied, "but sometimes I wish I could spend the same amount of time as others my age working on my own future."

"Jefferson, do you miss your grandkids?" I asked. "When I think of all the sacrifices you made, do you ever regret coming here so you and my mom could be together with me?"

"Boy, I never doubted that I'm supposed to be here and that you're supposed to be here."

He was proud of me and believed the Lord would bless me if I remembered that nothing was too great or too small to take on in this world. When we pulled up in front of the log cabin, the chickens were still asleep in the trees. Not even the poodle pack stirred. Somehow what Jefferson had said in just a few words made the early morning all right, put the daily trip to the Dungeness Inn in perspective, and made helping to support the family even better than okay.

In between working at the mill and the Dungeness Inn, I also took a course and studied for my real estate brokerage license. I wanted to have the option to sell local real estate. I thought deep down I could be a good salesman like Grandpa Whitey.

The highlight of the summer occurred when Whitey and Pauline, Ricky, and Patty came to visit. They had made it a tradition to visit every year in the late spring or summer. Sometimes they would stay for as long as a month. They would drive across country in their motor home, pulling a car or truck behind them, and Grandpa would sell the truck in Sequim to help pay for the trip. Grandpa Hughes was always ready to make a deal. I loved spending time with them. Besides my mom and Jefferson, Grandpa Hughes was my favorite

Ricky and Patty

person in the whole world. We would hook up an electrical cord from the cabin to the motor home. Then in the evenings around 8:00 p.m., when it was still light out on the Olympic Peninsula, Whitey and I would lie down in the motor home and read the latest *National Enquirer* tabloid article about how the aliens had been sighted or an article about the boy with the largest head in the world.

While Whitey and Pauline were visiting one summer, we drove the motor home west past Port Angeles to Neah Bay to go salmon fishing. Jerry, the boy from the detention center, was from Neah Bay. Coming here with Grandpa and Grandma made me think of Jerry and hope that he, too, had made his way in the world. Another weekend, the grandparents committed to taking me across by ferry to Seattle where I could sit for the real estate exam. That Friday, I had to work the night shift, so we left Sequim at 6:00 a.m. to catch the ferry. We barely made it in time for the 12:00 p.m. Saturday exam at a community college near Seattle. The exam lasted for several hours.

A week later the exam results arrived in the mail. I had failed by one point. I was so frustrated and disappointed; I knew I should have studied more. I thought, *if only I hadn't had to work all night the night before.* Why did this bad luck have to happen to me? Grandpa came upstairs to my door-less bedroom in the loft.

"Stop feeling sorry for yourself, Scottie. It just means you have to take it again. Never let your failures stand in the way and never blame anyone else. Remember to always focus on what you can do to make it right."

Grandpa helped me understand how important it was to not give up. I retook the exam and passed the second time. I even helped sell a piece of property and used the money for college.

After spending eight months working at the lumber mill, I finally arrived at the University of Puget Sound. During my time at the mill, I saved enough money to pay for one semester of college. Puget Sound was a prestigious small liberal arts school located in Tacoma, Washington. I was accepted for the fall semester. UPS was not as well known as Harvard, but it was often called the Harvard of the West. The campus was beautiful and what I imagined an Ivy League school would look like. Ivy covered the red brick buildings nestled under the Pacific Northwest canopy of the towering Douglas fir trees that surrounded the campus.

Jefferson was so proud of me and advised, "Boy just be yourself and know that you can make your own destiny."

If I couldn't land a scholarship or find a job, I'd have to drop out. My advisor, a professor in psychology, suggested that I only take one or two classes after reviewing my test scores. I explained that I only had funds for one semester and therefore needed to take a full course load. I chose history as a major and made all A's. After that, he always had a smile for me when I would see him on campus. Financially, I barely made it.

John Oppenheimer became one of my closest friends. We met in political science class on the first day of freshman year, and I remember seeing John surrounded by girls in the lecture hall. He came from a much different and well-to-do Jewish family, and he had the kind of personality you couldn't resist. When he was around, people gravitated toward him. John wasn't very tall, had lots of curls—which was the style at the time—and dressed real preppy, as if he could have been going to Harvard, which is where one of his brothers went. He wore a nice emerald green pullover sweater, white button-down shirt, and khaki pants complete with black loafers. In contrast, I wore jeans, a sweatshirt, and Frye boots, which I was proud of having recently purchased for college.

By spring of freshman year, John encouraged me to run for student body vice president. I thought he was crazy. It was not unlike high school, where one of the seniors convinced me to run. Oddly enough the slogan my college friends chose for me was "Action Jackson," just like in high school.

Student government helped pay for school. Eventually, so did many more scholarships and odd jobs. At the end of sophomore year, I ran for student body president. John signed on as my campaign adviser, and I won again. John volunteered as my codirector of public relations. As student body president, I served as the student representative to the university president's cabinet meetings and student representative to the university board of trustees. It was my job to translate. Sometimes I got it right and sometimes I didn't. I received the trust and respect from both students and the administration, because anyone could find me working day and night in the student union building.

Scott with fellow student body officers

I think if you work hard enough, even if you don't get it completely right, you earn the credibility to be heard. At UPS, I earned the credibility to be heard by all sides: students, faculty, administration, and even the trustees. There were major perks: My scholarship as a student body officer paid for room and board, and the president's executive assistant would even type my papers in a pinch.

The summer after junior year I was awarded a congressional internship in the office of US Senator Warren G. Magnuson. University of Puget Sound Board of Trustees Chair, Norton Clapp, supported my application for the internship. He also asked his stepson, Booth Gardner, to write a letter of support. Gardner would later be elected Washington State Governor. Another Congressman, Don Bonker, a Democrat representing the Third District, which included my hometown of Sequim, asked me to serve in his office, but Senator Magnuson's acceptance arrived first. That summer I left Washington State for Washington, DC.

I spent as much time as possible visiting monuments and museums and getting to know the city. I attended Senate hearings and frequently visited the House and Senate floor galleries. I promised myself I would return as soon as I could.

Beyond the internship and learning about the US Capitol, a girl who I thought was the most beautiful girl in college said she was going to visit me and see the sights in Washington, DC, and she did. Together, we saw much of the city. We went to the Smithsonian American History Museum, and we rented a paddleboat at the Tidal Basin for spectacular views of the Jefferson and Lincoln memorials. We saw the US Capitol by moonlight and its outline in the reflecting pool below.

She even stayed with me in the basement apartment I was sharing for the summer, since my roommates were gone for most of her visit. We slept in different rooms; nothing ever happened physically between us. We came from different worlds. She was raised in a well-to-do middle class home in Minneapolis, but our friendship made me realize that someone like her might someday be interested in a poor kid from Sequim.

During the weekdays that summer, I would often work into the evenings and then walk home at dusk from the Dirksen Senate Office Building to my small summer apartment located not far from the Capitol near Union Station. I wandered through several transitional and poorer neighborhoods, and I would see the homeless finding their spots on the park benches or up against the corner of a building to rest for the night. One evening I decided to stay out there with them. I bought a cheap bottle of wine and a package of little cigars, the kind with the plastic cigarillo tips, and shared both with those I met. Sleeping on the park bench made me realize that none of us, regardless of circumstances, deserves to be neglected.

On Saturday mornings, I would linger at the local park and watch the pickup basketball games. Everyone who played was African American. One Saturday I mustered the courage to ask if I could join them. After a pause and many disbelieving stares, there was a smile or two and I was added to a team. I wasn't very good, but I played all day and was one of the last ones to leave the basketball court.

Back at Puget Sound, I was reinvigorated. I didn't want college to end. I had grown to care about the people, and I knew they cared about me. Among the brick buildings and ivy vines, I felt safe and successful. I went on dates, had girlfriends, and on occasion I went to the fraternity and sorority parties. I would let down my guard and party with the best.

At the beginning of the school year, I was supposed to address the incoming freshmen during orientation week as their new student body president. Just before this, my good friend Scott, who had been elected with me as student body vice president—and who had recently returned from working on a fishing boat for the summer in Alaska—enticed me to come over to his dorm to do shots of tequila with all the beautiful freshman women. Scott was a resident assistant responsible for making sure the students in his dorm didn't get in trouble. I did the shots and then felt the effects as I walked with everyone to the stadium to give my remarks. I made it through my speech, but afterward I crawled my way into the stands to listen to the real president of the University and then blacked out.

The associate dean of students escorted me back to my room. The next morning, I called Scott to let him know that someone had broken into my room and broken the toilet while I was sleeping naked on the couch, and several inches of water covered the floor. He rushed over, and we both realized all of what had happened was my own doing. It made me remember what my mom told me the night I left for college.

"Most kids who go to college waste their education. They party and never do anything import-ant," she said. It was her way of try-ing to keep me headed in the right direction. I felt guilty enough to return to my studies.

With my closest college friends, I had shared my life story and how I got to the University of Puget Sound. My guy friends often wanted to come home with me during breaks to see the log cabin. One spring break, I brought four of my closest friends to Sequim. Whitey and Pauline were visiting, and Whitey served a delicious stew. He kept asking us if we liked it.

Yes, everyone liked it and had seconds and thirds. Then Whitey, with a smile on his face, told us we were eating horse meat he had brought from Missouri. I couldn't believe it. I was so embarrassed, but my friends took it in good humor. They didn't have any more help-ings, however. Jefferson got a big kick out of their reaction to Whitey and eating horsemeat. They were in awe of the cabin, but they were especially touched by meeting the Reverend Jefferson Jackson. They always wanted to spend more time with Jefferson and would even come with us to clean the Dungeness Inn and eat deli sandwiches.

By the time graduation arrived, it seemed a lifetime had passed since my days in Kansas. I woke up early on that Saturday. Jeffer-son was taking a rare day off work from the golf course (at least one of his jobs), and he and Mom were driving over that morning. Their arrival wasn't just important for me; Jefferson had been selected to deliver the baccalaureate sermon at Kilworth Chapel.

The service was set to begin at 11:30 a.m. By 10:30, they still hadn't arrived, and I began to worry. Two hours of one-lane high-way separated Sequim from Tacoma. This was only their second time visiting campus; their first was when I arrived as a freshman. As my panic increased, they pulled up. They gave me a pendant to wear on my robe that said "the world's greatest son" and a graduation card with lines from the poem *Desiderata* by Max Ehrmann. The words of the poem had meaning to me:

> *You are a child of the universe,*
> *no less than the trees and the stars;*
> *you have a right to be here.*
> *And whether or not it is clear to you,*
> *no doubt the universe is unfolding as it should.*

We rushed to Kilworth Chapel on the other side of campus. Inside the red brick building, we made our way to the front. Jefferson and I took our places near the pulpit. By the time the service started, hundreds of people crowded the pews behind Mom. Looking out, I saw John and Deanna, his girlfriend and later wife, and remembered that first day of class when we met. It seemed like yesterday and a lifetime ago at the same time.

I introduced Jefferson to the crowd. As always, he preached without notes. Even though he never finished high school, his eloquence captured the crowd with ease, truth, and passion. When he spoke to a nearly all-white audience about God, and how important it was to "love thy neighbor," people listened closely to this man's message of love and forgiveness.

After the service we proceeded to the main ceremony. I had missed my high school graduation by leaving early for New Zealand, so this ceremony assumed even more importance. University President Philip Phibbs and his wife Gwen had become my mentors and family away from home. I even lived one summer with another close college friend, Jeff Koontz, in the basement of the president's residence and served dinner to the governor of the state of Washington, among others, as part of my assigned duties. Still, I was shocked when President Phibbs addressed me directly during his speech:

Scott has distinguished himself in scholarship and leadership of the student body. Scott has been a partner to me and to the university in every way. Most significantly, there's no other student that I believe has made more of a difference to the university during my tenure as president than Scott Jackson.

I was overwhelmed. I looked for Mom and Jefferson in the crowd, and I thought about what we'd been through. I thought about the night I ran away from Dad. I remembered the abuse, and again I wondered what could have been, even more than what this mission had become. In leaving Dad, I chose Mom and Jefferson. But I also chose a childhood of paucity over a middle-class income and lifestyle.

Scott receiving his diploma from President Phil Phibbs

Scott and Jefferson at graduation

In running toward unconditional love, I unwittingly also ran toward economic hardship I never considered. Despite all that, I graduated with many honors. Still, I couldn't help but wonder if my achievements could have been greater had I not been forced to choose.

Imagining what life would have been like with Dad—or if my mom and dad hadn't broken up—was hard sometimes. It was in these moments I could imagine a happy family, playing basketball on the varsity team, and even having girlfriends who didn't run away after learning about my family. I imagined attending an Ivy League school. But then I wouldn't be Scott Jackson, Jefferson's number one son. I would be someone else, and I wouldn't have had Jefferson in my life. I knew I was where I was meant to be.

As graduation day drew to a close, Mom and Jefferson drove back to Sequim. Jefferson had to be at work by four o'clock the next morning. His "number one son" might have experienced one of the biggest days of his life, but the Dungeness Inn still needed to be cleaned.

Before he left for Sequim, Jefferson reached over and gave me a big hug, smiled, and said, "Boy, I am mighty proud of you. Know what they will remember about you is that your heart is the biggest they have seen."

CHAPTER NINE

Following My Dream

For all the closure college graduation seemed to bring, it carried with it just as many questions. Mom invited me to spend the summer back home, "helping Jefferson clean the Inn." Nothing could have put the fear of God in me more.

I'd been named an alternate for the post-graduate Rotary Foundation Ambassadorial Scholarship program, but it would be months before I knew if I'd travel overseas. Even if I did receive a placement, it would be a year before I actually departed.

Ideally, I wanted a job in Washington, DC. But without money, nights at the Dungeness Inn looked more and more likely. I applied for jobs at every egalitarian organization or government group in Tacoma. They all rejected me. I couldn't believe it: I was one of the most successful students in recent UPS history, and I was about to begin my post-college career unemployed.

Desperate for a solution, I organized a painting crew, together with my close friend Scott, and lined up more than a dozen jobs, mostly for faculty and staff at UPS. I rented a house near campus and spent that summer putting my newly minted degree to work painting houses.

Summer passed quickly. Each house presented its own challenges, but we never fell behind schedule. I bought an old Mini, whose brakes failed in the very first week, and traded it in for a small Datsun pickup truck. Besides, I reasoned, I could move my stuff to DC with a truck and sleep in back along the way.

All summer I thought about the plan John and I had put together near the end of school. He'd landed a job in DC and intended to rent a place with a second bedroom. John worked for a former member of Congress who had founded a small research institute that engaged members of Congress with corporations and other constituencies in their districts at conferences and through newsletters. The congressman also happened to own the townhouse in which John and I would be living. I just needed to get there by fall. And find a job in DC while working on the other side of the country. I was so set on DC that I even turned down a job as a UPS admissions counselor.

I had second thoughts, but I knew my dream.

As summer neared its end and I was painting my next-to-last house with my crew, Congressman Don Bonker called me. His district included Sequim. Even though I had chosen Senator Magnuson's office over his for my internship, Bonker still remembered me. Unfortunately, the congressman wasn't calling to ask me to DC. Instead, he wanted me on his Washington State campaign team in Olympia. I accepted a one-month volunteer position as his driver and reported for duty as the new paint on the last house dried. My first day on the job nearly ruined my career.

When I arrived in the campaign office for the first time, some of the staff seemed surprised to see me. The woman who ran the office welcomed me and began to introduce me as the congressman's new driver. A few minutes later, the door flung open and a young woman with dark curly hair bounced past. Her name was Gretchen, and she was in charge of the congressman's schedule.

"The congressman's already late," she said. "Here are the keys. The car is out front. Here are your directions. You're going to the Nisqually Delta."

She explained how the congressman was scheduled to accept an award for a housing grant he supported for a local American Indian tribe. A rival Democrat was also expected to be there.

"But this is Congressman Bonker's award," Gretchen said sternly. "So get him there first."

"Got it," I said. "Just two questions. Where's the congressman? And where is the Nisqually Delta?"

Right then Don Bonker walked through the door.

"Scott 'Action' Jackson. Good to see you. You made it."

That's all it took to get my blood flowing. Just like that, I was at the heart of a congressional campaign.

The congressman and I made our way outside and into the campaign car, a large LTD Ford that used to be his dad's. As we pulled away, I tried to forget how awful I was at navigating while driving. In fact, I wasn't even that great at driving.

The congressman directed me to the highway and north toward the Nisqually Delta. After we got off the highway, he seemed a bit lost.

"Go right! No, left!" he said.

His frustration came on suddenly and made me nervous. When I looked at the controls in front of me, I really became scared. For the first time since leaving the office, I realized we were low on gas. In fact, the needle was on empty. After a few more minutes of driving around lost, the car sputtered. When it jerked to a stop somewhere near the middle of the Nisqually Delta, I panicked.

At first, the congressman handled it well. When we turned on the radio, we both realized the severity of our situation. The local news was covering a story about a congressman receiving great accolades. It was Don Bonker's rival, accepting his award.

Fortunately, my days on the campaign trail improved. The congressman seemed to like having me around, and I was learning a lot about campaigns. I also met a bunch of interesting people, like George the sign man who drove a beat-up station wagon, with the back full of Bonker signs and a poodle in the passenger seat. The congressman was big on signs, and the sign man canvassed the district to deliver them to everyone in the third district who wanted one.

During my month on the campaign, I sometimes ran errands without the congressman. Once, he sent me to Sequim at the same time George was delivering signs in the area, so I invited George to the log cabin for dinner.

It was after dark before George found his way down the gravel driveway through the fir trees to the house Mom and Jefferson had built. I was always anxious when people arrived for the first time. Most of the friends I had brought during college saw the cabin as a fairy tale-like home in the woods. Its high ceilings and uneven floors held a quaint nursery rhyme quality they had never seen before. A few visitors, however, took one look at the place and couldn't believe anyone lived inside.

Since George had his own set of unusual qualities, I didn't think he'd be too surprised. Boy was I wrong. As the sign man walked to the front door carrying his poodle, I could see the shock register on his face. Inside, Moe the South American Macaw, with a wingspan of more than four feet, greeted him with a guttural cry while Super Cat, Mom's twenty-pound ball of fur and claws, attempted to draw blood. Also shocking to George was the pack of miniature poodle mixes that charged and began yapping around his feet. The pack represented what was left of three generations of litters—the descendants of Trixie—that Mom had chosen not to sell and were now allowed to rule the house. George clutched his own poodle protectively as Mom attempted to herd the dogs away.

The poodle pack had developed quite the lore around our house, mostly because of the incident with the rooster. Big Red was the biggest and meanest rooster we had ever raised. Jeffie-Lou and Shawne were both scared of him and would huddle together whenever he got close. Big Red was so large that we once hooked him up to a cart

and let him pull it along the entire parade route during the Irrigation Festival. So confident had Big Red become in his dominance
that he began to terrorize the poodle pack—that is, until the incident that day.

I forget who found Big Red hiding, but it quickly became clear that
the poodle pack had somehow organized an attack. By the time we
found him, Big Red was missing most of his feathers. He was never quite
so mean again. The poodle pack, however, gained so much confidence
that it started acting more like a pack of wolves than anything domesti-
cated. All this happened not long before George showed up for dinner.

Unfortunately, George never had dinner with us that night. Just
as Mom cleared her poodle pack from the living room, Jeffie-Lou
poked her head through the second-floor balcony rails. Jefferson was
in the kitchen, cooking something in a large pot.

"Cottie, you're just in time," she yelled out. "Daddy killed a rac-
coon and he's cooking it up for supper."

George's face went pale. He rushed out the door and back to his
station wagon, empty of all the Bonker signs he'd delivered earlier that
day. As he drove away, the poodle pack barked behind him.

As my month on the campaign trail came to an end, I told the
congressman I was leaving for Washington, DC. What little savings
I had was running out. I knew if I didn't go soon, I might never leave
Sequim at all. A permanent future with the poodle pack and Big Red
seemed far more likely than I wanted to consider. The congressman
stopped short of offering me a job, but said he looked forward to seeing me back east. We shook hands and I left the congressman's campaign office for the last time. A few days later, I packed up my red
pickup truck, complete with camper top, and hit the road.

Outside Ashland, Oregon, I pulled over for my first night on the
road and climbed into the back of the truck. As I fell asleep, I wondered if I had made the right decision. I had nothing promised and
everything invested in finding a job in DC.

As I made my way across the country, the Democrats lost many seats that first Tuesday night in November 1980. However, Congressman Bonker had won easily. For me, it was the only highlight of a night that also saw Ronald Reagan, the actor and former conservative governor of California, beat incumbent Jimmy Carter and become the 40th President of the United States. The election results also meant there would be fewer options for young Democrats in DC. After four full days of driving, with short nights spent at truck stops, I was within striking distance of the capital.

I entered the beltway approaching the nation's capital with the evening rush hour. Nearly two hours later, I parked in front of a townhouse on East Capitol Street, just two blocks from the US Supreme Court. John was inside hosting a farewell party for congressional staffers who worked for US Senator Frank Church from Idaho, a former Democratic presidential candidate. They had all lost their jobs in the wake of the Reagan Republican landslide. It had been one of the worst election nights ever for Democrats.

After the farewell party ended, John and I sat alone in the living room, eating leftover crackers and cheese. Just as he said he would, John had saved me a bedroom on the third floor of the townhouse. That night, my mind raced with anticipation. I barely slept. Almost two years since my internship in Senator Magnuson's office, I had finally arrived back in the nation's capital. Now there was one last hurdle: finding a job.

The next day, John and I planned to meet for lunch. Walking along the Mall, I once again felt awestruck by the grandeur of the buildings and monuments that stand at the center of American government and history. I arrived at Congressman Bonker's office a few minutes before 9:00 a.m. when the office officially opened. A

Washington State flag hung near the door. I entered a small recep-
tion area, and a beautiful woman with blonde hair welcomed me.

"Do you have an appointment?" she asked in a British accent that
startled me.

"No," I replied. "But I just worked on the campaign with the congressman, and he told me to come see him when I arrived in DC. I'm
hoping he can squeeze me in."

Another voice responded from behind me. "Congressman Bonker is in the office today, but he has a very busy schedule and a number of visits ahead of him," a woman said. "I'll see what I can do."

It was the congressman's executive assistant. She had just left the
congressman's office, closed the door behind her, and invited me to
wait. An hour later, Don Bonker walked out.

"Scott Jackson, you made it." The congressman sounded pleased
to see me, but his tone changed quickly. We walked from his office
to the House floor. Inside the US Capitol, frescos swarmed above
us. Small desks filled the room, and the podium where the president
delivers the State of the Union Address stood at the front. I knew I
needed to be a part of this.

Scott Jackson and his friend John Oppenheimer

"This is the worst time for Democrats in thirty years," Bonker said. "I don't have a spot open in my office, and former staffers from other offices are lining up for work, even if I could make room for someone."

I knew election night hadn't gone well, but I didn't realize how widespread the ramifications would be. The congressman left me at the entrance to the House floor and told me to return to his office after lunch.

In the meantime, I knew I needed a backup plan. I found my way to the office of Norm Dicks, the congressional representative who had beat us that day we ran out of gas on the Nisqually Delta. A couple of years earlier, I had hosted Dicks as student body president during a visit he made to the UPS campus. When I arrived at his office, his chief of staff took a meeting with me.

"Times are tough, Scott," he said, echoing Bonker. "We don't have anything right now, but let me think about it."

I walked outside and across the Capitol grounds. The office of Senator Magnuson was full of boxes. Staffers were packing their desks. Very few had any idea where their next job would be. I left before anyone could tell me again that it was the worst time for Democrats in thirty years.

John and I met for lunch at a place called Bullfeathers, named after President Teddy Roosevelt, located on Capitol Hill, not far from Congressman Bonder's office. At lunch, I looked at John in disbelief. Less than a day into my job hunt, it had become clear that my chances were bleak. John listened carefully.

"How'd you leave it with Congressman Bonker's office?" he asked.

"I'm going back there after lunch to continue our discussion," I replied. "Well, that's good," John said. "Now all you have to do is be yourself." Before we left, I asked the waitress for an application.

When I returned to Congressman Bonker's office, his executive assistant told me he was in meetings for the next few hours. I waited in the entry area until four o'clock. When he reappeared, he was in a hurry to get to a hearing. Again, we walked and talked. We made our way down the hall to the elevator. As we did, the congressman talked about staffing commitments that were already made.

"There's really nothing we can do right now," he said.

The elevator doors closed behind us, leaving us alone for the first time all day. I felt my one and only opportunity slipping away.

"Congressman," I said, somewhat loudly, causing him to look right at me. "I will work twenty-four hours a day, seven days a week, for nothing. Just put me on staff." I learned this from Jefferson.

He seemed surprised. My plea had caught him off guard.

"For nothing," he said. "You have to eat."

"Pay me what you can. I'll get a second job. Put me on staff and I'll do whatever it takes. There's nothing too big or too small."

The elevator doors opened and we walked in silence. When we arrived at the hearing, Bonker looked me right in the eye. "We'll talk after the hearing."

I sat in the audience and waited. When the hearing ended, we walked together back to his office. Along the way, he talked about the kind of work I would be doing if I joined the office. I could help with legislative correspondence, prepare meeting notes, help him get places on time, and do anything else other office staffers needed.

"It won't be glamorous," he said.

"It sounds perfect," I said.

At the office, I again waited in the entry area while the congressman spoke with his office manager. When she came out, she officially offered me the job.

"You're hired," she said. "We can pay you seven hundred dollars a month. Your job is yet undefined, but the congressman wants you on staff."

I could hardly believe it.

The congressman came out a few minutes later.

"I can't thank you enough," I said.

"We start at nine o'clock," he replied. "See you in the morning."

Scott with Congressman Bonker

The next few months flashed by. I wore a tie every morning and always arrived early. I sat at a small desk near the congressman's office. No two days were the same; order and predictability took a back seat to the issues of the day. I strived to respond with calm and helped however I could. One minute, I'd meet with constituents visiting from back home. The next, I'd drive the congressman across town. I learned the city quickly and always made sure there was gas in the car. I also helped keep track of his work with small businesses, the Department of Veterans Affairs, international trade, and humanitarian issues.

At Bullfeather's, where I had submitted my application that first day when John and I met for lunch, I was the only English-speaking busboy at the time. I also helped the congressman with odd jobs around his house.

I fell in love with Washington, even more than when I had been there as an intern. John and I made many friends and hosted parties. We went to lunch on the weekends when I wasn't working, read *The*

Washington Post, watched Sunday morning political commentators, and visited the Senate gallery during midnight filibusters. Washington quickly became my home. But almost as soon as I grew comfortable, the past came back into focus.

It was springtime when Dad called. I recognized his voice immediately. The last time we had seen each other was still that final day outside the courtroom in Port Angeles. I recalled watching him choke Mom and the day I ran away for good. Talking to him brought back memories I wanted to bury. It also made me wonder once again how my life could have been different, if only he had lived up to the words he used to preach. As our conversation wore on, my anger grew. I felt robbed of a childhood and opportunity. Whatever success I achieved came despite my family and financial challenges. The moral and spiritual support provided by Sydney and Jefferson had helped immensely, but it could never completely fill the void.

Dad and I had spoken only a few times in the past nine years. My mom had written a letter to my grandmother on my dad's side letting her know I was an exchange student in New Zealand. As a result, my grandmother had written to me to try to reestablish sporadic contact between Dad and me.

In her letters Grandma Agnes would tell me how proud she was of me, and then she would recount the details of their whereabouts and whatever was happening at church. She would almost invariably end with a sentence or two, or more, about Dad—how he missed me, how he needed me, and how he wanted to write himself, but that I should write him first. It was never about how he was sorry and how he wanted to support me—financially or otherwise. The guilt and the anger inside me would collide with the perseverance and the independence in my life and jumble it all together. Ultimately, I would need to find balance. The kind of balance Jefferson portrayed every day just to walk down the street. During our phone call, Dad mentioned that he and his second wife were coming to DC for a church conference, where he would also preach that Sunday at the National City Christian Church located on Thomas Circle.

"We'd like to spend some time with you," he said.

I didn't know what to say. It had been a long time since I had even thought about my dad. I hadn't yet forgiven him for anything that happened and wasn't sure I ever could.

"Let's play it by ear," I said, maybe because I didn't know how to say no.

As I hung up the phone, I knew I couldn't get out of it. I told John what had happened, and he offered to go to dinner with us. I was relieved. At least I wouldn't have to face Dad alone.

A couple of weeks later, Dad and his wife arrived at our townhouse by taxi. As they walked up the sidewalk, I had a visceral feeling about this. He looked as stern and disapproving as he had when he was bringing me back to Kansas. It wasn't fair. What I saw in him was everything I didn't want to be. The way he looked. How much he weighed. His mannerisms. Everything I saw made me angry.

I did my best to calm down and answer the door. We sat in the living room with John and talked for a while.

Dad grimaced as he sat down. He started to tell John why they were here and explained that he would be preaching on Sunday at the National City Christian Church. John asked more about his work with the church. The entire time all I could do was think about how unfair it was to be sitting in this living room, pretending that he was part of my life. Fortunately for me, John carried the conversation. More fortunate for me, we finally left for dinner.

We went to a restaurant in downtown Washington, DC, Charlie's Crab House, not far from the White House and the National Mall. We mostly made small talk. They never asked about Mom or

Jefferson, and they asked only a little about me. I had been accepted as a Rotary International Ambassadorial Scholar a few weeks earlier and told them as much. Dad offered to help with my overseas expenses but never followed through. I don't think I really expected him to.

After dinner we walked in front of the White House. They caught a cab back to their hotel, and John and I walked home.

John then casually said, "That wasn't so bad. They seemed nice enough."

I lashed out at my beloved friend. "Are you kidding?" I said. "How does he come here and pretend everything is okay or that there is nothing to ask forgiveness for?"

My balance was a work in progress.

After Dad's visit, I committed myself to work even harder and began to prepare for my year overseas. My acceptance as a Rotary scholar would send me to the University of Edinburgh in Scotland for an MBA. Things were finally falling into place. The cherry blossoms lined my morning jog along the National Mall, and I found myself feeling a bit nostalgic about leaving this place I had come to love. I wanted a degree that would stick and that would work around the world, and one that I could get in less than two years—and I had to have a scholarship. I didn't want to do something that wasn't well known or practical. The thirteenth-month program at Edinburgh fit all my requirements.

As spring turned into summer, I began to organize fundraising events for the congressman. Other Democratic members of congress began to notice me. Life was good.

Suddenly it was fall, and I had to leave for graduate school. When I arrived in Edinburgh, the cold Scottish wind welcomed me as if to acknowledge that everything I had heard about Scottish weather was indeed true. The day was cold and gray. It was September, and school, located in the heart of historic Edinburgh, would soon begin.

On the first day of class, I walked across a campus full of history and checked in with the business school. Each of my forty-member student cohorts had an assigned desk and locker. Every professor had his or her own office, and there was one lecture hall with smaller classrooms across the corridor from the professors.

I made my way to upper campus and onto the cobblestones of High Street. At the bottom of High Street stood the queen's residence. At the top, Edinburgh Castle. The postgraduate dormitory was a centuries old stone structure constructed originally to serve the castle. My room came complete with two roommates and a radiator that produced only eight hours of heat per a twenty-four-hour period.

The classes at the University of Edinburgh were the hardest I'd ever taken: statistics, microeconomics, macroeconomics, and marketing theory. Weekdays included six hours of class and a late lunch followed by six hours of studying and homework. I had only a few friends, including Kaka, a Nigerian who was nothing short of a genius when it came to numbers. Kaka was quiet and kept to himself by habit and also because of his "different-ness." He lived in the same dorm as I did on High Street next to the castle. After class, we would find ourselves walking back to the dorm together. I was one of the only classmates to reach out to Kaka. We started having lunch together on the way home, stopping at the student union building for a curry.

Just before the end of the first week of class, I received a call at the dormitory. A Scottish gentleman named Alex Wilkie was on the other end of the line. Alex owned a women's clothing store in town and would serve as my Rotary host father during my time in Edinburgh.

"I'll pick you up for Rotary tomorrow and then we can go to the club for a whiskey," he said, not asking any questions.

Alex and his family became my support group in Scotland. I told them all about my family, and we attended church together, enjoyed Sunday night dinners, and shared whiskey with haggis. Alex Wilkie reminded me of a Scottish well-to-do Whitey Hughes. He was confident yet kind. He enjoyed life but was generous to a fault. I never could enjoy the taste of Haggis, but the Wilkies were like family.

During this time, I also managed to continue my commitment to exercise, running four to six miles on most days. Scottish weather proved challenging, and strong winds followed by sheets of diagonal rain became part of my regular routine. So did short winter days and long damp nights.

The brutal exam system at Edinburgh also came as a jolt. Each student's ability to analyze a subject and make cognitive arguments about conclusions was judged without reserve. Worse for me, bad handwriting wasn't tolerated. My scores were so low after my first midterms that I risked not passing half my classes. I met with the professors, took their advice, and rededicated myself to studying even harder.

When Christmas arrived, I flew to Denver to visit my brother Shawne at National Jewish Hospital, where he was being treated for severe asthma. Shawne was now fifteen and his condition had worsened over the years. National Jewish Hospital accepted him as a patient without cost in the hope that they could stabilize his condition and improve treatment. Mom and Jefferson were also there, along with Jeffie-Lou. Shawne was glad to see us.

In Denver, heavy snow began to fall. A blizzard enveloped the city. Huge blankets of snow covered the ground, and the wind chill dropped temperatures to thirty degrees below zero. It reminded me of the night I ran away, and I was grateful to be warm and cozy inside. The airport closed. It remained that way through Christmas Eve. The blizzard kept the airport shut for thirty-three hours.

I returned to Edinburgh and to my daily regimen of school and studies. June arrived and my exams came in quick succession, three hours each, two a day, for three days. If I passed, I'd then be able to

Sequim mural of Jefferson and Shawne

return to complete a final dissertation and receive my MBA. When the exams came to an end, I had hardly a moment to relax. The next morning I boarded a plane back to the states.

When I returned to Edinburgh, I arrived just in time for the posting of final exam scores. Students gathered in tight clusters as administrators hung lists of names and scores. Mine came in well above average, which meant I passed and could proceed with my thesis.

Over the next few months, I completed my MBA. The following school year I finished a dissertation that focused on international trade. Afterward I traveled across Scotland, England, Germany, France, and Switzerland before returning to the states aboard the Queen Elizabeth II, the most famous cruise ship in the world at the time.

CHAPTER TEN

I'll Fly Away

I was on a business trip when the call came. It was Mom.

"Jefferson has lung cancer. It's terminal." I gasped as Mom spoke.

"What do you mean he has incurable lung cancer? How can that happen?"

"He had a cough and some chest pain, and he went to see Dr. Sims. They took x-rays. Then Dr. Sims came in and said, 'Jefferson you're full of cancer, I don't know what to do,' and he just cried."

I said, "Well, there's gotta be a cure. What happens next?"

"We don't know. We're sending him to Seattle to get some tests."

"How's Jefferson doing?"

"He's okay. Do you want to talk to him?"

"Yes."

"How's my number one son?" Jefferson asked when he got on the phone. "How are *you* doing?"

"Well the lord giveth and the lord taketh away."

We would take this challenge on together. I flew home as soon as I could. During the next few weeks, we took Jefferson to see specialists at the University of Washington. They gave him less than a year to live. They also offered an experimental radiation therapy reserved for patients with no other options. If it worked, the tumor would stop growing and possibly even shrink. It might prolong his life. But, the doctors explained, it could work the other way, too.

We drove home from Seattle and prayed. Jefferson decided to try the treatment. At first, the tumor shrank. Then it spread. The cancer metastasized to Jefferson's brain. Then to his spine. We checked him back into the University of Washington Hospital located in Seattle. Jefferson became paralyzed below the waist. It was a Saturday. I remember because he told me he wanted me to go back to Sequim to preach the next morning. I began to protest.

"I don't have a sermon prepared," I said. "I don't know what I would say."

Jefferson looked up from his hospital bed. It was the same look he used to give me when I was a kid and he wanted me to listen carefully. "You don't need a sermon," he said. "You need to prepare your heart."

Jefferson was able to be moved home for hospice care a few days later. There would be no further attempts at treatment. I drove the two hours up from Olympia, where I was the new Third Congressional District Director for Congressman Bonker, multiple times a week to help care for him. The church community and others around Sequim also helped. Mom and Jeffie-Lou and Shawne spent as much time as they could at home.

A steady stream of visitors flowed in and out of the cabin in the woods. Even in his dying, Jefferson was bringing people together. We moved his bed downstairs to the guest bedroom, which had more room for people to visit now that he was paralyzed. Jefferson officiated a wedding right there. He also started preaching again. Small groups circled around his bed to hear some of

his final sermons. Knowing they would lose their pastor soon, members of the Little Brown Church held Sunday services by his bedside.

I recall one Sunday in particular. We managed to get almost fifty people into his room. Another fifty filled the adjacent dining room. We had a gospel band and special singers. Jefferson projected his voice as loud as he could. By then, it was nearly a whisper. To me, it still sounded as beautiful as it had that first day inside Gethsemane Baptist.

During one of Jefferson's final sermons, a family that didn't normally come to church brought their children to the house to be baptized. It happened without planning. Someone carried a horse trough from outside to the edge of Jefferson's bed, and we filled it with water from a hose. I helped Jefferson as he tried to touch each child for baptism. I didn't even know their names.

Jefferson placed his hand on each of their heads and spoke the eternal words: "May the Lord bless and keep you. May the Lord shine His face upon you. In the name of the Father, the Son, and the Holy Ghost, I baptize you, and you shall have life everlasting. Go in peace, my children."

Through his suffering, Jefferson handled himself with courage, love, and humor, even near the bitter end when pain overwhelmed him and he could no longer speak. As his condition worsened, Mom remained by his side around the clock. Jefferson grew weaker by the day. Not once did he complain. As Christmas approached, I knew it would be Jefferson's last. I went to Sequim. Mom and I were so consumed by caring for Jefferson that we forgot to plan Christmas dinner. We dug out some TV dinners and ate together by Jefferson's bed. I remember Mom complaining about stomach cramps. Christmas and the New Year came and went. Jeffie-Lou and Shawne returned to school, and we settled in for the end.

Memories of Jefferson are vivid and fill a lifetime. His last sermon at the Little Brown Church before he was paralyzed was about Psalm 23 "Thou shall not want." His favorite bible verses—and there were many—were "Jesus Wept" and "Suffer not the little children let them come unto me." His favorite benediction: "Let the meditation of my heart be acceptable in thy sight Oh God my Lord and my salvation." His favorite attire during the week: blue overalls. On Sundays: a dark suit, white shirt, and tie.

Drawing of Jefferson with his parrot Moe by Steve Devine

Before he died, Sydney asked him, "Jefferson, is there anything you would want different?"

His last words to the love of his life were, "Only that we would have had more time together here on Earth as I will love you for eternity."

On February 8, 1986, Jefferson fell into a coma. A doctor visited. Jefferson had already decided he wanted to die naturally at home, and he wouldn't use a respirator or otherwise prolong his life. That same night, Mom collapsed. An ambulance took her to the hospital. She had severe intestinal blockage. With church members filling the house, I divided the next day between the log cabin and the hospital, as Mom underwent surgery. We moved Jefferson's bed to the living room so more visitors could surround him. He remained in a coma, his breathing faint.

That night with the house nearly empty, I went upstairs to rest. A single church member stationed by Jefferson's bed called my name a few minutes later. I rushed downstairs. Jefferson had motioned slightly with his hand. I sat down beside him and placed one of his hands inside my own. I began to speak.

"Jefferson, it's Scottie. I love you. Mother's okay. Jeffie and Shawne are here with me. We all love you. I love you. I hope you know how much I love you. It's your turn to be at peace. Thank you for all you have done for everyone, especially me. Thank you for teaching me that there is more than anger in this world. I will always try to do good and make you proud."

Jefferson let out the final gasp of air still left in him. Then he was gone.

Reverend Jefferson Jackson died early in the morning. I later learned that Mom woke from surgery at the exact same time. A few days before Jefferson slipped into his coma, I received a call that my paternal grandmother had died. Dad wanted me to come for the funeral. I told him I couldn't. I was forced to make a choice between two families. I chose Jefferson.

Jefferson's funeral took place at the Little Brown Church. Mom dressed Jefferson in a long white robe with golden slippers. Pat Wright and the Total Experience choir performed. Attendees packed the church and flowed out the door into the yard. I sat in the front row with Mom, Shawne, and Jeffie-Lou. I delivered the eulogy and talked about the influence Jefferson had on my life and so many others. I recalled that first day at Gethsemane Baptist when Jefferson's singing overtook me. I talked about our cross-country escape and how Jefferson and Mom fought for my custody in the face of violence and racism.

Jefferson was our rock. My mom loved Jefferson. Jeffie-Lou and Shawne loved Jefferson. I loved Jefferson. Without him, I might never have grown to look beneath the color of a person's skin. Without him, I might never have known that a man doesn't need to be filled with violence and anger to earn respect. Without him, I wouldn't have stayed close to God. He taught me that each of us has a chance to impact others simply by being the best people we can be. He changed the lives of everyone he touched.

After the service, a long procession drove from the church to Sequim View Cemetery. At the gravesite, we all sang "When the Saints Go Marching In." Jefferson was one of those saints. As his body was lowered into the ground, tears flowed and we released hundreds of multicolored balloons into the sky. The closing hymn at the burial was "I'll Fly Away," as the balloons turned to tiny dots, carrying the lyrics, floating above, fading to silence.

> *Some glad morning when this life is o'er, I'll fly away;*
> *To a home on God's celestial shore, I'll fly away.*

Our beloved Jefferson died too early at age sixty-four. Jefferson's grave marker is inscribed on a roughly hewn field rock: "Beloved Husband, Father and Pastor." I chose the name Scott Jackson because I wanted to model my life after Jefferson. It was how he treated others regardless of how they treated him. It was how he truly lived his faith . . . "forbearing and forgiving one another". . . Christ-like.

While I often wondered if my life would have been easier if my parents had stayed together and my father had given me more opportunities in life, I now know that without Jefferson's influence, I could have been a different man—a man more like my dad. Jefferson taught me that it was better to love than to hate. He showed me how to choose forgiveness, to treat women with respect, and to accept people with a different color of skin as equal, even as family. His greatest gift was that he loved me unconditionally.

Jefferson Jackson lived almost his entire life in small towns. He was undereducated and didn't finish the tenth grade. He died with very few material possessions. He was ostracized because of the color of his skin. Yet, through his faith and goodness, he left a legacy of hope for all those he touched and for generations to come. His favorite song and my favorite to hear him sing was "I Wonder Do You Love the Lord Like I Do." The meaningful words of this song and the heart and passion with which Jefferson sang them are positive messages I will never forget and try every day to live by. They encouraged me to choose a career path in philanthropy.

> *I wonder, do you, love the Lord as I do. What he gave to me*
> *was given to you.*
> *Are you staying here content. Will your soul some day repent.*
> *Will you show a child the way. Will you do your best even*
> *in distress.*
> *Will you do some good each day I wonder, do you.*

Jefferson saw very little of the world. But he changed it for the better.

Jefferson Jackson's grave marker

CHAPTER ELEVEN

Leaving a Legacy

J efferson Jackson may not have traveled the world, but his influence led me to ultimately choose a career path that would not only lead to visiting more than sixty-five countries but also engaging in meaningful work that would help others in need throughout the world. I kept my promise to him that I would always try to *do good and make him proud.* Jefferson was always there for young people, offering support and guidance to any child in need. I took that to heart and decided to be a force for good to other kids, the way he had been for me.

I worked for Congressman Bonker for half a decade, focusing on international trade and development issues. Another father figure came into my life unexpectedly during the Bonker 1988 US Senate Campaign. It was Gary Gayton, born February 25th, 1933. He was the fourth child of John and Virginia Clark Gayton and the grandson of Seattle pioneers John T. and Magnolia Gayton, one of the first African American families in Seattle.

Gary was a star athlete in track at Garfield High school and the school's first Black student body president. He was the first member of his family to attend college. He went to the University of Washington, majored in political science, and excelled in athletics. He graduated with honors from Gonzaga University Law School in Spokane, Washington. Gary's distinguished legal career began with an appointment by Robert Kennedy as an assistant US attorney. He was a successful civil rights attorney for African Americans and Native Americans in a number of hallmark cases.

Gary came into my life when he agreed to be the Finance Chair for Congressman Bonker's 1998 US Senate Campaign. Gretchen Sorensen had worked with him and knew how amazing he would be as our Finance Committee Chair. I in turn served as the Finance Director, and I too soon found him to be amazing. One of his iconic phrases was "Here's the deal." Gary's love and joy for life was contagious. He was also connected to everyone in Seattle, and we were not. Gary and I became joined at the hip in our efforts to raise funds and awareness for the Bonker Campaign.

Gary reminded me of Jefferson, even though they were very different people. Jefferson never made it past the eighth grade, whereas Gary completed law school with honors. They each chose to love others every day regardless of how they were treated or the prejudice around them.

We didn't win the campaign, but Gary remained a mentor and inspiration in my life. He and Gretchen are the godfather and godmother of my three girls. It was almost as if Jefferson brought Gary into my life so that I would have a father figure who would help me continue to choose love in how to treat others, regardless of the circumstances.

After Congressman Bonker left office, I formed my own public affairs and marketing company, which included Congressman Bonker, called Tradec (Trade and Development Consortium). And for the next decade, I worked in international public affairs in the private sector, opening new markets in developing countries, before accepting a position at World Vision and moving over to the humanitarian side. At World Vision I helped design programs that would engage our donors and traveled around the world to work with our teams on the ground. I then went on to take a leadership role at PATH, which focused on global health, such as procuring and providing an affordable meningitis vaccine, MenAfriVac®, for Africa.

Now, as the President and CEO of Global Impact, an organization focused on changing the world by growing Global philanthropy, I'm still involved in raising funds and awareness to meet critical humanitarian needs around the world by providing corporations and individual donors with effective ways to donate to international causes and crises. Global Impact's mission is to raise resources for the world's most vulnerable people, and in this capacity I still get to work with World Vision, PATH, and many other international relief and development organizations. In conjunction with our member charities, we work to end hunger, improve prenatal and childhood health care, supply clean water, deliver medicine and other disease-prevention programs, build schools and train teachers, help with rescue efforts following a disaster, and much more. Over the past decade before the great recession, the United States and many other governments have increased public and private sector support for development tenfold. As a result, we have halved child morbidity and mortality, we have actually started to win our assault on deadly but preventable diseases like malaria, and we have turned the tide on the HIV/AIDS pandemic. Yet there is so much more work to be done.

My work has been a surprisingly transformational journey—while I've witnessed firsthand its positive effect on others, the very people we have helped have also had a profound impact on me. I have seen the best in people in the worst conditions and have been deeply moved by their courage and perseverance. So many people helped me when I was a child, and now I've had the privilege of traveling the world and meeting other kids like me.

One of my early trips with World Vision involved co-leading a pastors' trip to the West Bank and Gaza. World Vision was raising funds to support children because it was a conflict-torn area. Some of our donors had supported Palestinian Christians, but many were not fully aware of the dynamics on the ground. I don't think any of us had a real understanding of what was occurring in the Palestinian territories. Our trip was during one of the Intifadas when Arafat was still in power. I had no idea that Palestinians were in such dire straits and being held captive through a series of checkpoints. The checkpoints were every so many hundreds of feet inside Gaza or the West Bank, and if you didn't have the right identification, you couldn't travel past the checkpoint. Palestinians might have a day pass to go to work during the week, but then they were unable to pass the checkpoint on weekends to shop at the grocery store. Towns were literally divided in half.

During our visit, we realized that people were being held here in severe conditions. While inside the West Bank, I stayed with a family that World Vision was sponsoring, and their son gave me a tour of the town. His ability to marry would depend on whether or not he was able to own land and build a home, which under the circumstances was highly unlikely. Everything became affected by the situation they were in: school, nutrition, livelihood—even the ability to marry and have a family. We visited a checkpoint with Palestinian guards where the previous night the Israeli army had mistakenly shot a donkey on that side of the sand bank.

"What if we just go back inside the checkpoint here?" I suggested nervously to the boy who was both my host and interpreter.

We also visited a school for the deaf in the Gaza strip that was supported by World Vision. Because it was so difficult to have a normal community development model, World Vision provided aid to existing institutions, and our visits helped us to determine their funding needs.

Suddenly, an outbreak occurred in the street with gunshots. This provoked the Israeli army on the other side of the boundary to start firing their weapons, and bullets began whizzing by us. We were on the rooftop of the school for the deaf, and we grabbed the students and marched them downstairs. We tried to transport them safely to their homes through difficult streets, doing our best to avoid the gun-fire. The donors and pastors on our trip were all transformed by what they witnessed. Hopefully, we gave some hope to those we visited.

Children at the school for the deaf in Gaza

Scott with Rich Stearns, President of World Vision, in Gaza

I will never forget our World Vision trip to Guatemala. We were bringing donors out into the communities where World Vision was working to show them our programs in action, and the sponsorship coordinator urged us to visit a family who had recently lost their daughter. Even though this little girl had received support from World Vision, not every child makes it—a lesson that remains with me today. For every billion who live on less than two dollars a day, many drink bad water, and many of those people die from preventable causes, such as diarrhea. We read about statistics every day, but sometimes we forget that behind that statistic is an actual real, live, human person. Even if we're able to help hundreds or thousands, we are painfully aware that so many do not survive, and they leave behind grieving families.

I met Lesbia Arana, who had lost her daughter Marcia to lupus nine days earlier. Through her tears of grief, Lesbia recounted Marcia's long and painful struggle against her disease, and her need to obtain more and more treatments. Many parents in Guatemala were turned away from doctors because they were poor. World Vision provided Marcia with the best treatment available in the region, but it wasn't enough. We should have been able to do more and we all felt it. Marcia was yet one more statistic, one more child out of so many who would never realize her potential.

What made this particular trip so meaningful was the opportunity I had to engage with Lesbia and how she connected with me. Toward the end of her story about her daughter, I got up out of my seat and put my arms around Lesbia.

"You did everything you could," I said. "She's with the Lord now. We'll take her story back with us and tell others. We won't forget her."

Even though Marcia had died, we could still take her story and do something with it. She could serve as a reminder of how far we had yet to come and why we needed to remain committed to this work.

The success stories are important because they give us hope, but the kids who don't make it serve as a haunting reminder.

———————

When I was working with PATH, I took a trip to Vietnam with a group of donors. We were there to see the work PATH was implementing around the country. PATH is an organization that works with pharmaceutical companies around the world and creates health technologies for low-income communities, simple things that could be used in health clinics with minimal training. They had just invented a vaccination syringe that could be used by anyone, not only medical professionals, which would enable more people to receive vaccinations.

We visited one health clinic in a community where PATH had been involved with training. It was vaccination day, and there was a nurse on site. At least one hundred women were lined up, and each held her child's vaccination card. They were there to receive the vaccinations for that particular month, and people had traveled from rural communities in Hanoi in the northern part of Vietnam. We entered the clinic and observed the vaccinations and then saw the sharp waste. In addition to the problem of people reusing needles, they often discard needles in places where no one will take them away and safely dispense of them. In many cases, huge piles of needles accumulate and form treacherous mounds next to these clinics. Kids play with them, and it's a nightmare.

PATH invented a system for detaching the needle from the rest of the vaccine, cutting down waste, and then stacking the needles within a container that could hold thousands of needles—like a big barrel with a top that had a special opening for the waste. This container could then be buried in the ground as a way to safely eliminate this waste and protect people from getting hurt. These seemingly small inventions can have a huge impact on health and safety in developing communities.

I pulled the nurse on staff aside and said, "Can you tell me what impact PATH has had on your clinic? What else can we be doing?"

She replied, "PATH has brought life-saving vaccines to our clinic. PATH has trained us and given us the tools and equipment to have a well-running clinic to serve more people. And, finally, as a result, PATH has helped to make our community healthy and prosperous."

The PATH trips were a bit more indirect, because we weren't actually running the clinic itself. The work of PATH was more about training and developing appropriate technologies in health that could then be implemented in communities where it was needed. But it was important for donors to see firsthand how PATH was improving people's lives. The donors were appreciative of the experience and it affected each of them differently. Some were struck by the fact that it had helped communities, others that children were kept alive.

As a father, it was important to me to share some of these experiences with my daughters. I wanted to broaden their perspectives and show them how other people lived around the world. I also wanted to impart the lesson that helping those less fortunate was a valuable action and something they could aspire to in their own lives.

While working at World Vision, I had the opportunity to take my eldest daughter Lindsay, who was about twelve at the time, on a medical boat that traveled up and down the tributaries of the Amazon River in South America. For many villages, the only regular medical care they received was from one of these medical boats. We lived on the boat for a week, along with some of World Vision's donors. We witnessed everything from standard vaccination days to more severe heart attacks and strokes, as well as triage for the sick. The boat would stay overnight in one area and then move on to the next community the following day.

From this experience, we all began to comprehend the real importance of health care, especially for kids. It was interesting for me to see my daughter Lindsay realize the significance of having clean water in a place that had very little drinkable water and take an interest in testing the water. We recognized the juxtaposition of the breathtaking Milky Way at night and lush environment during the day with the stark contrast of so much pollution due to a lack of sanitation. But Lindsay's real epiphany would come on our next trip.

A couple years later, I took the family with me on a trip to Africa, including my three daughters. We started off in South Africa and then traveled to Zambia and Kenya.

We visited a small Catholic hospice dedicated to people dying of AIDS, unable to receive life-saving treatment because of poverty. Once HIV was contracted, there was no hope. Their final days were spent at this hospice. The first two rooms contained orphaned babies and toddlers, and we held the babies in our arms. The reality of their condition struck all of us, especially Lindsay. They were alone, dying, and there was no hope of treatment; and yet they still managed to express happiness through their laughter and singing. In the final two rooms, adults occupied each bed and all available floor space. Emaciated, sick, and saddened faces peered at us from above their meager blankets. One man had traveled a great distance to die alone, so as not to be a burden or stigma to his family and village. We were also able to see some of our work in action in the Shipanuka community in Zambia, where we celebrated the funding that had given them a new well and latrines. We all had a huge feast together, and then they took us to see the new wells. We did a ribbon cutting for the latrines, and they introduced us to two twin girls who were the same age as our twins.

The Jackson girls meet twin counterparts from Shipanuka, Zambia

In a hotel in the capital city of Lusaka in Zambia, Lindsay had a life-changing experience. It was early evening, and Lindsay was in the room, freshening up before dinner, when an African house-keeper entered to clean the room. As she began to empty the trash, she pulled out a candy wrapper that had been discarded by one of the twins, with a couple pieces of candy still remaining.

The woman looked at Lindsay and said, "Do you mind? Are you going to eat this? There are two candies left inside. Why did you throw them away?"

"No, I don't mind," Lindsay replied. "My sisters threw it away."

"If you don't mind, I will take it home to my children because they don't have candy. We don't have food to spare here, and every little bit counts."

In Africa, most people live on less than a dollar per day. This inti-mate one-on-one encounter made Lindsay fully realize what this meant. What many of us discard in life, someone else can hold precious.

The Jackson girls, Lindsay, Haley, and Allison, surrounded by the children of Shipanuka, Zambia

When I moved over to the humanitarian side, I saw things I would never have seen otherwise. These experiences helped me to see the human face of our work and why it matters to children around the world. What drives me is that while in some respects it feels so far away, from my own childhood I know that what other people do to create opportunity means that kids like me get an education, medical care, and what they need. I never had to live on a dollar a day. But I did grow up in a tenuous house where I felt real fear as a child, and when I finally escaped I was confronted with racism and poverty. I worked hard to improve my circumstances, but the generosity of so many people helped me along the way.

As a kid it really meant something to have others express confidence in me and to believe that I had potential. I was grateful for the programs that allowed our family to make ends meet or enabled me to have an education. The opportunities I received because of the generosity of others, as well as the institutions for social good, had a real and lasting impact on me. There are so many children in this world who come from broken homes and don't ever have the chance to realize their potential. Some don't even make it to school or receive any type of health care. Because of the positive influences in my life like Jefferson and my mom, I learned to view life with a sense of optimism and to do my best regardless of circumstances. As an adult I've chosen to love people and be positive—and my own childhood has caused me to be drawn to marginalized people around the world.

I don't think it's a coincidence that I've met so many other kids like me during my travels, children who were around the same age that I was when I made my own escape. I'm not looking for credit— that's not important to me; I only care about what we all accomplish to help these children. I believe that each of us will be measured by what we do or don't do to eradicate extreme poverty so that every child can realize his or her potential. I know firsthand how important that is. We all have charity within. For me, I want to leave a legacy that's about choosing love instead of anger or hate.

Women members of the microcredit farming cooperative in Swaziland

CHAPTER TWELVE

Full Circle

orty years to the day, I traveled from Washington, DC, to retrace my steps when I ran away from Linwood, Kansas, in the snowstorm in order to return to Sequim, Washington. I was now in my mid-fifties, my hair no longer blonde, now much darker and sprinkled with shades of grey. I had just endured a significant foot injury and surgery, and I made the journey on crutches with a boot still on my injured foot. My first stop was the Claycomo farm, Whitey and Pauline's home, where I had fond memories of eating hamburgers and drinking chocolate shakes and where we had all gathered to decide where to flee to escape the custody suit. The next stop was the barn, and then the store.

The store was now a much more dated thrift store. The McDonald's where Ricky and I used to escape to still stood on the corner across from the store, and that is where I ate a late lunch. I then visited Grandpa and Grandma's grave site at the Liberty Christian Church, where Sydney and Don had started their lives together, where Pauline had written sermons for every minister who served, and where Whitey always made sure to add generously to the offering plate.

Before leaving Claycomo for Liberty, I found my way to see Bill Edward. His home overlooking a lake with ducks and other wildlife was familiar, though the house also showed signs of wear. Bill had been my rescuer those forty years earlier and then continued to be there for me whenever I needed him. I had even borrowed money from Bill for my business. Bill now owned the Claycomo Hughes family farm. He was glad to see me. He was fighting cancer, which would take his life six months later. We both knew it would be the last time we would see each other.

He said, "Scottie, Whitey would be so proud. He always believed you would do great things. Committing your life to others would make him proud—that was what was most important to him."

He confirmed his recollection of the night I ran away and was hidden in his attic. We hugged, took a picture together, and without many words affirmed the greatest gift anyone can give—kindness to another. He had been significant in my life; he made me better. I loved him and he knew it.

The next morning, I set out just before sunrise in the midst of a cold Kansas winter. Snow covered the ground but no blizzard conditions like there had been forty years earlier. After driving across the Missouri River, I made my way to Edwardsville. My first stop was the First Christian Church. Then on to the little parsonage house, which was even smaller than I remembered. A train sped by and I realized that we really had lived close to the tracks. I visited the farm Mom and I once owned and where we had hoped to remake the rest of our lives. A large mansion had been built on the property. People said the owner had brought the stones from England.

To my surprise, the original tin-roof barn was still standing. The trailer where we lived was long gone, but the tack room—once our living room—was now where the owner kept chickens. I could still imagine the piano with the broken ivory keys that I would play and where I would spend hours practicing hymns and writing my song for my mother.

I visited Gethsemane Church where Jefferson preached, and though it was now abandoned, it felt to me like yesterday, the church full of people, deacons with their white gloves and Jefferson's booming voice. I could imagine the outline of the cross that had smoldered at the entrance of the farm.

I made my way to Bonner Springs and saw the high school where Mom had taught, remembered some of the students, and thought about Michael. Linwood and Tall Oaks was closer to Bonner Springs than I remembered. The little town had fallen on hard times, and the post office where Dad had kept me from getting my letters was now boarded up. The school was still there and the front parking lot where I had once pleaded with my mom *take me with you.*

Tall Oaks campground just outside Linwood was in better condition and looked much the same. The house I remembered was much grander than in reality, but it was still livable. I introduced myself to the current caretaker and knocked on the door at the side of the house, where my Dad had kept his office and his secrets. Whether it was race, religion, the times, my mother's independence and intelligence, or just a bad combination of two young people who never really had a chance of staying together, when I look back as an adult, I have a more comprehensive understanding.

Dad had been raised to want a submissive wife, and Sydney Lou was never going to be that.

Part of it was what he had learned from his own father, but another part stemmed from his jealousy of Mom, because they were so different and she was so outgoing and likable. It isn't all about race or about abuse—it's about what each of us does with all that. I have realized that life is short and that the opportunity to forgive is not forever.

I turned to the reason I had come in the first place: to retrace my steps on the night I had run away. Every step from the house to the camp lodge became real again. The pay telephone was no longer there.

Across the meadows, along the tree line, past the swimming pool to the open air chapel, on to the cliffs overlooking the Kansas River.

The cliff seemed higher and farther away. I put the crutches back in the rental car, drove around the campground, and picked up the trail by the meadow adjacent to the cliffs. I stood in front of the meadow and pictured where I would have gotten the thorn in my foot. I could see the path down the cliff all the way to the railroad tracks along the river. I crossed the bridge to DeSoto and made my way to the horse ranch.

In all, it was a twelve-mile journey. I didn't know what my life would be like the day I chose to run away and reunite with my mom and Jefferson, but it has been an extraordinary journey.

CHAPTER THIRTEEN

To Gulu and Back

The humanitarian trip to central Africa that I led in late 2005 had the most profound impact upon me. It was the center of a vicious and horrible civil war between the people of Northern Uganda and the Lord's Liberation Army (LLA), led by deranged warlord Joseph Kony. More than 1.5 million Acholi were considered internally displaced persons (IDPs) and for their own protection were forced to live in overcrowded refugee camps, enduring squalid conditions. They lived in constant fear of invasion of their villages and communities by the young, brainwashed warriors of the LLA.

Kony was known for raiding villages before dawn, abducting young boys into submission to become soldiers, raping girls, and forcing them into slavery until he discarded them later on the trail—beaten to death or maimed beyond recognition. Beatings alone did not suffice. The LLA made its mark by lopping off the arms, legs, breasts, noses, and ears of the victims. They especially practiced these brutal methods of control on the young girls and children. To avoid these atrocities, the families in the surrounding villages and region encouraged their children to make their way into the city of Gulu, where the United Nations and the participating nongovernmental organizations (NGOs) maintained secured compounds with separate makeshift barracks for the boys and girls.

The "night walkers," as these school-aged children were known, made their way into the city before dusk to study by flood lights, sleep, and then by the first light of dawn return to their family homes for a meal of meager proportions. These children then traveled to the village school, and the cycle began all over again. This nightly ritual continued as long as there was known LLA activity in the region. Kony and his child soldiers sought refuge across the border in Sudan, where the Muslim extremist government seemed to tolerate their ungodly cause. Over the past twenty years, the LLA has captured, brainwashed, maimed, or discarded for dead more than twenty thousand innocent children. These children are the unlucky ones. The lucky ones—the night walkers—simply lived in fear. But they lived.

I arrived in Kampala, the capitol of Uganda, after a long flight and taxi ride from the Kampala airport to downtown Gulu. The rest of my delegation, which consisted of Rotarians, donors, and community leaders who wanted to witness World Vision's work, arrived late that same day. The Seattle delegation was a unique group of individuals. They had recently witnessed polio vaccinations in Ethiopia. But nothing they saw in Ethiopia, nor anything I had seen in the more than sixty-five countries and difficult places around the world I had traveled to, could have prepared us for what we experienced in Gulu.

The next morning we boarded our chartered bus outside the hotel for our journey to Gulu, two hundred miles north. It was a bumpy ride. We encountered more frequent checkpoints as we headed north. The final checkpoint on the long, winding road before we reached the city took a long time. Government soldiers surrounded the bus. Two boarded with their machine guns visible, briefly speaking to the driver, deciding whether or not our delegation could continue. We realized that the conflict here, while deep-seated, was also very real and evident. We were finally allowed to proceed but only after one of the soldiers had walked up and down the aisle and was satisfied that the contents of the bus, including the delegation members, were not to be worried about.

Our hotel in Gulu was rudimentary, even compared to Kampala, with clean rooms but no electricity or hot water. The beds sported mosquito nets, an important amenity during malaria season.

We spent the next several days learning, listening, and witnessing the results of the war atrocities firsthand. We also saw the hope for a better future in the faces of the Gulu children and people we met—those who had been left behind. Women were still not outside of harm's way in the massive refugee camps, as many were raped inside the camps as a matter of course. We met with Acholi tribal leaders who were powerless because they were significantly outnumbered against the well-armed LLA young vanguard.

Our delegation had an extraordinary experience visiting and spending the day with the maimed, disfigured, but ever so hopeful women taking refuge in the World Vision Children of War Rehabilitation Center for former child soldiers and the women and young girls who managed to escape the LLA. The center provided them with food, medical treatment, psychological counseling, and vocational training, among other things. These children came to the center before they would then try to travel home to their villages, many of them traumatized and lacking the ability to reintegrate themselves into their communities. Some of them would never be able to live independently or return to their family homes. Some had babies; some were just kids.

I met a young woman whose nose had been cut off. One of her breasts had been sliced off and she was missing an arm, with only a stump in its place. She was only twelve or fourteen and had been fetching water when the army captured her and forced her brother into military service. But she was still alive, and I saw the love she carried for her son, the bastard child of one of the men who had raped and maimed her. She sat down on her bunk in a small room with her baby on her lap and began to tell me her story through an interpreter.

When she was captured, she was raped multiple times and then given to a much older soldier as a trophy bride. One night when the soldiers weren't paying much attention, she tried to escape. They cut off her nose, breasts, and ears, so that she would be too ugly and damaged to receive help. She gave birth to a child but never knew which soldier had fathered it. A few months after she gave birth, fighting erupted and the LLA army was losing, so it retreated and she fled. The Uganda government army rescued her and brought her to the World Vision rehabilitation center in Gulu. There were a million other refugees. I told her she was brave and beautiful—truly beautiful inside and out. She smiled and thanked me. She would do more than survive. World Vision would see to that.

We then went outside and took a picture of our delegation with all of the women because they wanted us to. We listened intently to their stories and spent time with them, just as others had been with me during my difficult times. These women had been through so much—and yet they had endured and found their own charity within, including love for their fatherless children, born out of violence and rape. As they shared their love, we shared in return. We felt joy for the triumph of the human spirit.

Later that afternoon, the World Vision staff had arranged for me to visit my sponsored child, Simon Ojok. World Vision is the largest child sponsorship agency in the world. Simon was only one year older than my twin girls, Haley and Allison, and three years younger than my oldest daughter Lindsay. The girls, when they were still young, had chosen Simon's picture when we decided to sponsor a child while attending our first World Vision Child sponsorship concert in

Scott with a child at the World Vision Children of War Rehabilitation Center

September 2000. It was during intermission, and we selected Simon in war-torn Northern Uganda. Or perhaps as I stood in front of a photograph of Simon and his family, he picked us.

We sponsored Simon for more than a decade, during most of his precious and precarious childhood. Every year we received a picture of Simon and a report on his progress. And every year I had been thankful that he was still alive. Now I fully understood the real possibility that Simon could easily become a victim. Simon could have been a night walker. His brothers and sisters, who were older, could have also been night walkers.

Simon lived in the nearby village, and we drove an hour to visit him in our white Land Rover with the bright orange World Vision decals on the side. As we drew closer, the roads began to give way to rough terrain. Finally, we pulled up to a hut with a grass roof, and Simon and his mother and brother came out to greet us. Simon lived with his siblings and his mother—his father was no longer living. He was very shy and I shook his hand, as the interpreter told him who I was and he in turn expressed his appreciation. I explained that my family had been supporting him for a long time, helping him get to school and receive medical help. He told me that he wanted to be a construction worker. First he had wanted to be a teacher, then a construction worker, and then a hairdresser. When he completed elementary school, he asked World Vision to help him pay for vocational school—he wanted a profession so that he could take care of his mom, who had become HIV positive.

They invited me into their hut, and his mom was so proud of having us there. Simon pulled out a box that contained a few of the letters we had sent him over the years, so I knew he understood who we were. I had brought some school supplies, books, clothes, a soccer ball, and a Polaroid camera—simple gifts for a family who needed so much. It had been all I had been able to carry with me. It reminded me of when I could only bring my deflated basketball, when I had been forced to determine what was most important to me and what I would have to leave behind in my efforts to escape my abusive father. Everything we do counts for somebody.

Simon is now more than 21 years old. We continued to help sponsor Simon during vocational school, until his mother became ill and he was required to return home to support her and the family. Sadly, we have recently lost track of Simon. When we met in person that time, it was somewhat awkward. And yet there was a connection that we could not deny. Simon was a survivor and so was I. Simon, though a seemingly ordinary boy, was—by staying alive, staying in school, and supporting his mom—without knowing it, living an extraordinary life as a model for all of humanity. At one point Simon sent me a letter that I will forever cherish. It was not unlike the letters I have sent to the people who have looked after me, the individuals who saw something in me that triggered the charity within them. Without their help, I would not have made it across the country to be with my mom, I would not have finished college, and I would not have had an opportunity to provide for my family and try to make a difference in the world. Simon's letter sent on October 3, 2012 reminds me of those letters and those significant others in my life:

Dear Scott,

First of all I would like to send my greeting to all of your family members. How are you out there? It has been a very grateful happiness when I and my mother heard that you sent school fees. It has been a God plan for me to have school fees. I always put my trust in God as the Bible says. God has done a great miracle for in my life to have studies and I promise that I will never spoil my opportunity to do so.

Honestly, I received the money and paid for my fees and also I bought with the fees other school requirements such as a ream of printing paper, A4 figure log table, a drawing board, T-Square, a mathematical set, half a dozen of 96 page exercise books, 3 meter tape measure, 3 kgs of welding rod, 10 hacksaw blades (eclipses) 18 teeth per 20 mm, 3 drill bits (size 4), and 6 toilet rolls (required for boarding students).

Scott, thank you for your cooperation over my studies. Please send my greetings to all your family members. I have to stop here thanks. Blessings to almighty God.

Thanks,
Ojok Simon

Scott with Simon and his family

The war was at a precarious state. Every night was different. Some nights there were few night walkers and the streets were relatively empty; other nights when the LLA activity was sighted nearby, there were many thousands of child night walkers. That evening our delegation would walk in solidarity with whoever walked to Gulu in search of refuge.

The streets of Gulu were filling with hundreds, even thousands, of children as the Lord's Liberation Army was active in the region. It was somewhat frightening to be surrounded by so many children at dusk making their way to the safety of the camp compounds inside the city.

Then suddenly I felt a tug on my left side. I looked down and a little girl, perhaps eight or nine years old, was trying to get my attention by pulling on my jacket.

She took my hand and said, "My name is Rose. Take me with you." In my own childhood, every day when my mother would try to escape the abuse, I would plead with her and say "take me with you."

She smiled at me, continued to hold my hand, and we moved together with the mass.

Rose and I, along with the rest of our delegation, made our way, seemingly pushed along by the crowds of children into the football stadium with the large gates that would soon be closed behind them to keep them safe. Inside the stadium, high fences encircled us and floodlights illuminated the compound. There was someone on a high-rise stage at one end of the field with a microphone and a record player hooked up to the loud-speaker system that surrounded the stadium. The young leader on stage explained that the children needed to make room for those who had exams the next morning—to allow them to be close to the light to study before lights out and curfew would require them to head to the separated barracks for their few hours of sleep.

Suddenly I heard a beautiful chorus of a thousand voices move through the crowd. It was hard to make out what they were singing at first, although these hymnal tunes were familiar to me. Uganda is a predominantly Christian country and many of these children obviously had great faith. These thousands of children who had little to sing about were bursting out in song. A powerful emotion swept over me, as I recognized the words of "Blessed Assurance." *This is my story, This is my song, Blessed Assurance all the day long.* This was the same song the all-white congregation had sung at the Edwardsville First Christian church where my dad preached. It was the same song the children had sung at Gethsemane Baptist Church on the other side of the tracks in Edwardsville where Jefferson preached. It was the same song that Jeffie-Lou, Shawne, Sydney, Jefferson, and I all sang at the Little Brown Church in Sequim. How could this be? All these worlds, all these different cultures, all these different children—all of us connected by a hymn, by our faith, and by each other.

These children, the night walkers, validated my journey to date and affirmed my way into the future. During the same time that Joseph Kony was terrorizing the children of Gulu, I continued my own path. Not unlike the night walkers, my own escape became the door to a more promising future.

Without the other people in my life who chose to show me love, I too would have been a victim.

I saw Rose only once. She disappeared into the night and compound with the other children. But because of Rose I remember every day that there are children all around the world who must overcome the struggles in their lives and choose the love within rather than the anger. Each of us can be the other in their lives and help them make that choice and make the world a better place.

Make Your Global Impact

For me, sharing my story with others and the influence my upbringing has had on why I care about making a global impact has made it more personal. Recounting my story to different audiences made me realize that we all have a story to tell and these goals are not just about the larger world—they are about each of us realizing our full potential as human beings and understanding the ways we can be intimately connected to the goals through our own stories.

Throughout the years at dinner parties, meetings, prayer groups, and small gatherings of friends and strangers, whenever I was invited to tell my story, I was always amazed at how people responded and wanted to know more about how my childhood has shaped the work I do today. So I began writing a manuscript . . . not knowing where it would lead.

More recently, I have been bold and taken the risk of sharing my story with larger audiences both through a published book and speaking engagements. The impact my life story had on people has been part of my own journey of "Making the Global Goals Personal." It has led me to want to make a global impact, to support the Global Goals for Development, and to be an agent for positive change in the world.

It was emotionally moving for me to realize that divulging my personal story and why I cared about the Global Goals was meaningful to others, which is why I am sharing my story with you. My story is about a boy from a broken home who struggled to become a person with purpose. A boy faced with racism and violence as acceptable ways of life. A boy who finally found his future by having the courage to follow those who loved him, regardless of their social standing or race. It is also the story of millions of children in the United States and around the world whose own journeys from brokenness and inequity required the courage to escape from their conditions and have a better future.

When we look back on our lives, will we have heard and responded to those children who called out "take me with you," loudly or quietly? Were we the significant "other" to a person in need? This book is also my call to action—especially for the millennial generation and generation Z, whose destiny is not only to be connected but also to change the world for the better. You are not bound by race, culture, language, or geography. You are confident, connected to the world, and open to change.

My narrative is rooted in adversity but also in love and faith. It is about finding the charity within and resisting the anger that can overtake everything.

Each of us has a story to tell. Some of our stories are of difficult circumstances and struggle, and others are of love and nurturing and perhaps for all of us a combination of those experiences. Your journey—and your story—is important.

Regardless of where we are born and the struggles we encounter, we all have the opportunity to choose a love for others. To choose a life of service. To be someone else's other when they are making some of the same choices. Each of us can make a global impact. Choosing service to others in our daily lives is not just about how we show up and the impact we can have in the world—it is also about the example we set for others.

How I've Been Impacted By This Work

With more than twenty years of experience in international development, working at World Vision, PATH, and Global Impact, I've witnessed firsthand some of the most pressing issues that we face globally. My travels to developing nations have had a profound effect on me, increasing my awareness and compassion and reinforcing my determination to make a difference in whatever ways I can. I have also seen the extraordinary efforts of non-profit organizations, foundations, corporations, governments, and everyday people like you and me, who are stepping in to help find innovative solutions. So many people in the world struggle for access to health care, economic opportunity, and gender and racial equity. We must all confront the impact of climate change around the world. I now know just how important it is to protect women from violence and trafficking and to provide them with education and economic opportunities. I have seen children who are suffering because of violence, hunger, and disease. Everyone deserves a chance to live without extreme poverty or the threat of violence or prejudice because of the color of their skin, and we all must do our part to eliminate these global challenges.

EMPOWERING WOMEN

More than fifteen years ago, a close friend and colleague at World Vision, Kathryn Compton, asked me in my capacity as a Senior Executive if I would sponsor a luncheon in New York to increase awareness of the plight of women and girls around the world. At that time, we wanted to focus on the impact HIV AIDS was having on women. I agreed, even though the world was only beginning to pay attention to the issues affecting women in the developing world. Today, Strong Women, Strong World™ is a thriving campaign, an empowerment movement of women of faith to raise resources and awareness of issues, such as HIV AIDS, economic improvement, violence against women, child marriage, water and sanitation, maternal and newborn health, and girls' access to education.

Women account for more than 50 percent of the world's population, and yet they suffer disproportionately from domestic violence. How often does a man raise his voice or hand towards a woman because he can? Like my mother, women who are abused physically or even emotionally are led to believe it is somehow their fault. They fight back in their own way sometimes, taking even more abuse for the sake of their children.

One in four women will experience domestic violence in her lifetime. Domestic violence is most likely to take place between 6:00 p.m. and 6:00 a.m., and it is the third leading cause of homelessness. More than four million women experience physical assault and/or verbal abuse by their partners. More than three million children witness domestic violence in their homes every year. Children are more likely to intervene when they witness severe violence against a parent, which can place a child at great risk of injury or even death. Currently, the lapsed Violence Against Women Act has not yet been reauthorized, leaving victims in the US unprotected from domestic and gender-based violence. Unfortunately, we have seen an increase in domestic violence in the midst of the Covid-19 global health and economic crises.

The majority of human trafficking is of women and girls, and it is growing, not diminishing, around the world, with billions of dollars representing its not-so-underground industry.

Every year more than fifteen million girls are married as children and denied their rights to health, education, and economic opportunity and are robbed of their childhood. In rural Kenya I once witnessed with my own eyes the ceremony following the tradition of genital cutting of a twelve-year-old girl. She stood in the middle of the village for over a day as she waited to be betrothed to a man four times her age. As a result of this forced marriage, that little girl will never realize her full potential, and the rest of us will miss out, not knowing what she could have really contributed to her family, her community, and the world.

Without access to family planning for women, other essential interventions to reduce poverty and inequality will be far less effective. Every year 300,000 women suffer a preventable death during pregnancy and childbirth. Women produce half the world's food but own or have legal rights to less than 1 percent of the land on which they produce that food. Two-thirds of the children denied primary education are girls. One hundred thirty-two million girls around the world are not in school. When girls are supported in school, they become women who contribute to a better society that benefits everyone, including boys and men. Organizations like World Vision and International Center for Research for Women (ICRW) have made it their business to provide essential services for women and girls and break the cycle of poverty for half the world's population.

Advocating for the Forgotten and Runaway Children of the World

My three daughters mean the world to me. I have lived, and I will die, believing they are the most precious gift I have ever been given. I have worked hard to make sure they never have to experience what I did as a child. Lindsay, the oldest, and her identical twin sisters, Haley and Allison, are all three like stars in the sky for me. We are forever thankful that they grew up with all the love and care we could give them.

Unfortunately, millions of children throughout the world still need our help. There are children who are neglected, kids in less than ideal foster-care situations, and young adults on the run. There are also children in developing nations who are malnourished, dying of preventable diseases, and at risk for being abducted and raped or forced into armies as child soldiers.

Thirteen percent of all young people under the age of eighteen live on less than $1.90 per day. It is estimated that about fifteen million children live in poverty in the United States. That number is even higher throughout the world. About three in ten African American households with children are unsecure. On average, 15,000 children in the world under five years of age will die each day, and more than half of those deaths are caused by preventable diseases, such as pneumonia and diarrhea. More than six million children will die every year from such causes.

Globally, malnutrition contributes to about 45 percent of the deaths among children under five years old. One out of every five children under five fail to meet even basic dietary standards. Between the year 2000 and the present day, more than thirteen million children under eighteen have lost one or more of their parents to HIV AIDS, and three out of four victims of malaria are children under five.

While these numbers may seem staggering and overwhelming, there is so much that each of us can do to make the world better for children. We can give our time, and we can donate to the programs that are implementing real concrete solutions in some of the areas that need them most.

We cannot forget our children—they are our future.

As you read in chapter thirteen, the invisible children of Gulu known as the "night walkers" were forced to leave their homes and villages each night to find safety in the camps until morning when they returned and attempted to attend school. For more than twenty years, these children and their conflict remained unchecked—and invisible to the rest of the world. Like the forgotten children in other parts of the world.

The children of South Sudan and the Democratic Republic of Congo continue to be raped, turned into child soldiers, or forced into servitude. Human trafficking of children for sexual exploitation and forced labor represents an industry with more than $150 billion in annual profits, the third largest illicit industry after drugs and guns. Of the estimated forty million people held in slavery around the world, as many as eighteen million of those are in India alone, and ten million of those victims of slavery and indentured servitude are children.

In the United States there are an estimated two-and-a-half million homeless children, 48,000 juveniles are incarcerated in youth detention facilities, and another 500,000 youth are brought to detention centers in a given year. More than four hundred thousand children are in foster care in the United States.

Of the 5.6 million Syrian refugees, it is estimated that more than half are children running away from war without a place to go. Another 6.2 million people are displaced within Syria, including 2.5 million children. Palestinian youth in Gaza and the West Bank turn to violence because they cannot find a livelihood, own land, or marry.

In the Central American countries of El Salvador, Guatemala, and Honduras, where half the population lives below the poverty line, there are more than one million forgotten children who are trying to escape to the United States or other countries to find a better life. Many of those who don't escape, or who are forced to turn back, join drug cartels and gangs as their only means of livelihood and survival. Tragically, more than 5,400 children have been separated from their parents at the Mexican border since 2017.

Between the ages of ten and thirteen, I too experienced what it was like to be one of the runaway children held hostage by social prejudice and family violence. I was forced to run away to find my future. It's important that we do whatever we can to help children on the run—from war, violence, or abuse—to find safety and security.

More than 1.4 trillion dollars is spent on education, and yet Black students have only a 79 percent high school graduation rate, and Hispanic students have an 81 percent rate in contrast to a 92 percent rate for Asians and an 89 percent rate for Caucasians who complete their secondary school education. Thirty years ago the United States was ranked number one for the amount of people receiving secondary education diplomas. Today, the US is ranked twenty-first in the world for their high school graduation rate.

De Tocqueville in his observing of American culture wrote: "It cannot be doubted that, in the United States, the instruction of the people powerfully contributes to the support of a democratic republic." Yet, today 1.3 million US secondary student don't graduate on time. Fifty percent of those who attend college will take six years or more to get their undergraduate degree.

Worldwide there are an estimated 258 million school-aged children who are not in school. Girls represent more than half of those not in school. Two-thirds of illiterate people in the world are women. In Sub-Saharan Africa, 11.7 million children leave school before completing primary education, and those numbers have increased as a result of the Covid-19 global pandemic.

Of those fortunate enough to attend secondary school, it is estimated that for every year of secondary school completed, a child's future earning potential increases as much as 25 percent. Access to safe schools, trained teachers, adequate school supplies, and tuition fees is a proven and essential formula for breaking the cycle of poverty. Children born to educated mothers are less likely to be stunted or malnourished, increasing their odds of having healthy and productive lives.

When I was studying in the University of Puget Sound Collins Library, alone with the works of philosopher Reinhold Niebuhr or enveloped in the study of the Civil Rights Movement, I learned that the great equalizers are education and knowledge. No socioeconomic class can take away what you learn. Even more important is what you can do in the world with such knowledge. For today's young men and women alike, we can't afford not to invest in their education. The cost of not investing is simply too great. Everyone deserves a decent education, and it's important for the advancement of our entire world that we make significant strides in education globally and work diligently to reduce the number of children who do not receive even a primary school education.

From Story to Impact

Making a global impact starts with reflecting on your personal story. Examine the narrative that has shaped the person you are today and identify the voices crying out for change—maybe it was you or maybe you were witness to someone else saying, "Take me with you . . . take me to a more promising future, a better life." Then direct your charity from within toward the mission of helping those voices, giving hope to others reaching out for a better life.

For me, my global impact included reflecting on and retelling my story to hone my life's work of advocating for the forgotten and runaway children of the world, empowering women, and standing up for global causes at large. Motivated by my story, my global impact has taken many forms, but for someone with my past, it might look like advocating for, volunteering with, or giving to organizations.

I encourage you to explore your story and use it as a catalyst to make a global impact. I have the privilege of leading a passionate organization where we believe everyone can be an agent for positive change in the world. We would love to be a part of this journey with you. You can visit charity.org/globalimpact for a collection of inspirational resources and storytelling tools to guide your path. By harnessing the power of our individual stories and weaving them together, our global impact will be even greater. I hope you'll join me as we carry out this important work for those asking to "take me with you."

Make Your Global Impact

Take the pledge to make your global impact.

Share your story at charity.org.
Commit to causes you care about.
As a global citizen, advocate for justice and equality.
Support the Global Goals for Sustainable Development.
#makeyourglobalimpact

Consider Charities to Support

Consider which charity you would like to actively support. For instance, you might choose to become involved in the Strong Women, Strong World™ movement to transform the lives of women and girls who live in poverty in developing countries. This is an initiative of the charity World Vision that aims to empower, protect, educate, and nurture women and girls living in some of the most challenging places in the world. The United Nation's Global Goals for

Sustainable Development

I leave you with a call to action. You are the generation of global citizens who will and *must* meet our global challenge. The sworld is calling you. And you have the opportunity to change the world.

Your journey—and your story—is important. Go forth as global citizens. Answer this call to action by sharing your own story with others. Get engaged with the Global Goals for Sustainability and make them personal. Become an advocate for eliminating extreme poverty, rejecting inequality and injustice, and preserving the environment for future generations.

Join the ONE Campaign to Make Poverty History (http://www.one.org/us/). Become a Global Citizen (http://www.theglobalcitizensinitiative.org/). Give to a cause you care about. Be a game changer and establish your own Growfund Giving Account (https://mygrowfund.org/). Contribute to the Global Impact Sustainable Development Goals Fund (charity.org). Take action by committing your time, talent, and treasure to a better, safer world.

Acknowledgments

For those who have been willing to let me share my story, you have been my inspiration, and I am grateful to you. For the many heroes in my life who, when I shared my story would encourage me to share it with others, I am deeply thankful. For all those who have committed your own stories to making a difference in the world, I want to express my gratitude to you for inspiring me to pursue my work.

Putting my story into words has been a long journey. Making it relevant to the world we live in and the world we want is essential. I want to give a large thank-you to my editing team who helped me shape the story so that others might see themselves in it. I am especially grateful for the work of the talented Lara Asher who took on the task of the final editing and completion of my manuscript. I want to thank Carol Mann and the Carol Mann Agency and my publisher Kenzi Sugihara, President of SelectBooks, who each took a chance on an unknown author for my first book and are now publishing a revised and updated version of my memoir.

I want to extend great gratitude to Rich Stearns, President of World Vision USA and author; Dr. Chris Elias, President of Global Development for the Bill and Melinda Gates Foundation; and former Congressman Don Bonker, my mentors and friends who wouldn't let me stop until the story was told. I owe a big thank-you to John Oppenheimer, for being like a brother to me and always willing to read the next version of the manuscript. My gratitude to Scott Burns and Gretchen Sorensen, my good friends, always ready with a word of encouragement. To my family, who have endured the impact of this story, I have great appreciation for my mom and Jeffie-Lou, who have never left my side, and to my three daughters and their mom, who are all on their way to change the world in their own journeys.

I owe a very special thank-you to my wife and partner, Patricia.

I also feel a great gratitude for my wonderful friends and colleagues at Global Impact who have continued to support me in this endeavor: May Samplonius, my executive assistant, Steve Polo, Global Impact Board Chair, the Board of Directors for their support, and all of the Global Impact staff and extended family who have made their own pledge to make a global impact.

Finally, I want to thank all the young men and women of future generations who continue to inspire me because they have chosen to find the charity within themselves and have chosen to make a global impact.

About the Author

Photo by Elizabeth Dranitzke

SCOTT JACKSON is the President and Chief Executive Officer of Global Impact. Global Impact's mission is to grow global philanthropy and build partnerships and resources for the world's most vulnerable people. It has raised $2 billion since inception. A global development fundraising and marketing veteran, Jackson has held leadership positions in the public, private, and nonprofit sectors, including the global health and development nonprofits PATH and World Vision. He has worked in more than sixty-five countries, and his global relief and development efforts have taken him to remote villages in Africa and Asia, to the heart of the Holy Land, and inside some of the most powerful institutions and governments around the world. Jackson has worked with global leaders around the world. He has worked on international development programs with four US presidents and their administrations.

Jackson was a founding member of the nonprofit organization ONE Campaign to "make poverty history" and has worked on initiatives with Bono and the Bill and Melinda Gates Foundation. He is a long-standing member of the Clinton Global Initiative, and he serves on several national boards, including the International Center for Research on Women and the U.S. Fund for UNICEF. He currently works closely with the leadership of more than one hundred twenty nonprofits around the world, such as Save the Children, CARE, and Doctors Without Borders. He has traveled to Uganda to raise awareness about war criminal Joseph Kony. Beyond Africa, Jackson has assisted with major relief efforts in the West Bank and Gaza Strip, in New York City after 9/11, in New Orleans post-Katrina, and in Manhattan after Hurricane Sandy. He's worked to fight famine in North Korea and preventable disease throughout the developing world. Jackson has led Global Impact's efforts to raise resources for the COVID-19 health crisis, racial and social injustice causes and organization, and the economic impact that the world is facing.

Jackson has worked on global poverty and global development issues with many individuals and organizations, including Nelson Mandela, Desmond Tutu, Al Gore, Saddleback Church's Rick Warren and Focus on the Family's James Dobson, and civil rights leaders Jesse Jackson and Al Sharpton. He's a trusted and influential behind-the-scenes voice, whose opinions and insights have spanned political, religious, and racial divisions and helped shape policies at the highest levels for more than three decades.

Before taking leadership roles in the global development humanitarian sector, Scott founded TRADEC (Trade and Development Consortium), one of the first marketing and communications firms in North America to specialize in international trade and development, which later became part of APCO, a worldwide communications firm. During his early career, Jackson served as assistant to a US congressman, and he held a number of roles in national politics. He has appeared in *The New York Times*, *The Washington Post*, and *The Huffington Post*.

In October 2016 Jackson was awarded the Gelman, Rosenberg and Freedman CEO EXCEL Award by the Center for Nonprofit Advancement. The award recognizes leadership achievement in the areas of innovation, motivation, community building, ethical integrity, and strategic leadership.

Jackson received an MBA from the University of Edinburgh School of International Business. He also holds an honorary Doctorate of Humane Letters from the University of Puget Sound, where he received a Bachelor of Arts in history. He lives in Washington, DC.